G000243326

Finding Black Gold on the Emerald Isle

by Willetta Fleming

©2014 Willetta Fleming. All rights reserved.
No part of this book may be reproduced in any form
without the permission of the Author.
ISBN 978-1-291-82638-8

I dedicate this book, and work of love to my mother Diane and my late father Gus.

I honor their lives. I honor the selfless decision they made to give me life, not in conception but by choice.

Also I dedicate this book along with my heart to my two little stars Grace Diane and Adrienne Joy. You both shine deep rich beauty, and it will change the world forever.

Acknowledgments

I give my lasting gratitude to my life long mentor Mrs. Karl
who told me I could.

To Cherith for your wisdom and your time.

Thanks to all my wide array of friends from school mums
to church folk, it is all of you that have made this island home.

Finally to anyone who has given me your words, it matters,
whether face to face, handwritten or typed. I thank you.

Foreword

Willetta Hassenrik Fleming

We knew from the beginning she was a special child of God. She came to us as a very small, happy baby. As she grew, so did our love for her. Those beautiful penetrating eyes and darling ringlets of hair framed her bubbly personality that won the affection of everyone around. In school, she was so cute the teachers had difficulty disciplining her. We, her church family, watched as year after year her artistic gifts began to flow. No child could be loved and admired more than our precious Willetta.

She always knew she was adopted but often had questions about why her birth mother had chosen to give her to be raised by a specific Caucasian couple. One day at school she said to me quite out of context: "My mother hates me." At first, I was confused. I knew her custody parents loved her dearly. Only later did I realize she was referring to her birth mother. In spite of moments of feeling rejected, she continued to thrive in the home God and her birth mother had chosen for her.

A few months after Willetta was born, I met her birth mother briefly at church and was touched by her sparkling personality. A few years later, at the request of Willetta's custody parents, I visited her to discuss changing Willetta's status from legal custody to adoption. At that time, her ears were closed as she still had dreams of a better life. However, after a series of events, I sat with Willetta outside the courtroom while the final adoption took place. Afterwards, although they had only met a handful of times, they embraced and tears were shed. Her birth mother had given Willetta the freedom to soar.

God answered prayer and protected Willetta from being sucked into a life of drug addiction, prostitution, and imprisonment. Although the forces of evil continue to devise plots to draw her into the kingdom of darkness, that kingdom shall not win. She is God's very own--called out of darkness into His Kingdom of marvelous Light.

In this book, you will embark on an emotional journey with Willetta as she takes you on a trip through her experiences in and out of darkness. Some parts she writes about are factual. Other parts are open visions that help interpret the seasons of her life.

This author's writing will grab your attention as well as your heart. She is well on her way to fulfilling her destiny. Won't you come along with her?

-Pastor C. Yvonne Karl, D.Min.

Preface

I was a born Romantic.

The Emerald Isle as far as I knew had people with a sing-song accent and girls with flowing hair as red as fire. Little did I know that the people residing in this beautiful country of Northern Ireland also had a preconceived idea of me as well.

The moment this became apparent was probably within my first few weeks of living in a small city outside of Belfast. Immersed in new wedded bliss, I was walking around still in my fog of having just moved to a country which most Americans long to visit in their lifetimes. Bam! Like a punch in the stomach after eating a great big meal, it came! They were a cute couple that fitted my stereotype of a little old Irish couple; that is until the words came out. They sort of scrunched up their faces, in a *lets see if she can understand us* way. They proceeded to say very, very slowly... "Hi Ya, what island do you come from?" I began to search my brain as to what they might mean. Island? Surely this was my first time on their Island. I responded very politely, "I am from

Michigan." They looked at me, then each other, trying to figure out what I could be meaning. They then proceeded to explain to me they had visited Africa on mission many years ago.... From the word Africa in their sentence, my mind realized it had found the missing puzzle piece for my confusion and theirs. I came back into focus as they stared. I said once again, "I am from Michigan, in America!" As quickly as they found me intriguing, they became unamused, almost as if I had burst their bubble. They nodded and wandered off down the quaint little street.

It was from that day on, I began to realize my idea of the quaint little fairytale Emerald Isle and its idea of me were going to crash big time.

Chapter 1

I was born African American to a drug addicted mother. Failing to change her lifestyle of incarceration and drug abuse, she asked the people who offered her help to look after me. I lived with and was eventually adopted by a wonderful Caucasian couple with whom she had entrusted me. Eternally grateful for the beautiful life I was given by my adopted parents, my idea of race and sense of where I fit into my skin has been an interesting journey to say the least.

Beauty filled my life as a child. I belonged to an especially kind and warm church family. I attended the private Christian school that was part of the church as well. My circle was snuggly enclosed for the first twelve or so years of my life. In the summers, my parents and I traveled to our summer cottage in the Upper Peninsula of Michigan. Idyllic, but unnoticeable to me at the time I suppose, blueberry picking, painting at the children's art club, fishing, swimming in Lake Michigan and trips out on our sailboat would all be regular summer activities. Michigan has beautifully hot summers and, being the Great Lake State, the water is vast and refreshing.

My parents brought me up with a "spare the rod spoil the child" ethos. With a strict upbringing and a Christian faith at the root of anything to do with anything, they felt the need to protect me from outside worldly influences that inevitably presented themselves. I remember Mom recording Doris Day's *Pillow Talk* on the VCR off the television. Not only would she delete the commercials so we did not have to watch them on video, but anything she considered a bit risque she deleted as well. My parents were older when they adopted me so the old westerns and musicals were what I was familiar with on the entertainment front. Heavy petting or cursing was not allowed for my viewing pleasure. Of course, I craved glimpses of the kissing scenes. Mom and I would end up in fits of laughter as I peeped through my fingers, even though she told me to keep my eyes closed, as she muted and deleted faithfully.

I remember growing up with a lot of laughter. Although, when I look back now, I know my mother's laughter was usually out of sheer exhaustion at my dramatic antics. I was full of life, music and color. Everything I did was not short of theatrics. I remember one of my favorite movies being *Anne of Green Gables*. I pretended to be the main character, Anne. I pictured myself with red hair and Irish fair skin, dotted with hundreds of little freckles, getting up to mischievous adventures and having crushes on boys. I imagined leaving my romantic and special mark on the world. These were some of the ideas and childhood daydreams that painted my world.

The absolutely riveting experience of being adopted is an experience of unseen magnetic love that can bring family members to the surface.

Possibly due to my parents older age, I never got to meet my grandparents, their parents, as they had passed away before my arrival.

God ever true to His Word brought forward Aunt Sylvia to step in that empty place. Aunt Sylvia was my mothers' aunt, so technically she would have been my great aunt.

I knew she loved me since the beginning of my living with mom and dad. It was later from the age of six and up that formed my first thoughts of this woman who stepped into Grandmother role, perfect in her affections for me and her spoiling me silly.

Sylvia was a short woman, perhaps shrinking in her older age, and I remember she was soft and round perfect for hugging. I remember the drive to her home felt long because she lived in the city of Detroit. I would get bored easily and mother amused me with games of I Spy on the way. I did not grow up in a big city, so I contained curious wonderment whenever we would arrive in Detroit. She lived in a big house that also spiked my daydreams. One of my first memories is that she always kissed me, her lips were hardly in existence, yet she kissed me. I remember wiping them away because of their wetness. Both of us giggling after the kiss and hug, she would say, "Hold out your hand." Every time I held out my hand she would place money inside of it and then close my hand tightly, quickly glancing at my mother saying, "Now this is for you, get something nice ok?"

I have concluded that she should take part of the responsibility in my deep rooted romantic nature. She was intensely in love and utterly captivated by her husband, the very love of her life. To this day I have never seen a woman so very enamored with her spouse. I vaguely remember her dear husband who fought valiantly in World War II. I do sadly remember vividly attending his funeral and peeking around the corner to see my father and mother gently pull her away from her love's lifeless body. As a young child I felt my heart sink at the sight of that goodbye, not even fully grasping its depth.

Aunt Sylvia was very sad for a long time after his death. I think my mother brought me around a bit more often just to make her smile, and smile she did, every time holding on a little bit longer to each hug because her heart was broken in grief. Sylvia and her love only had one child my mother's cousin, Cindy. Cindy sadly never found a love to replicate her parent's strong example. Never having any children, she recognized her Mothers delight in this little black girl who won her heart.

As I got older I remember wiping her wet kisses off with a quicker stroke than before and swiftly holding out my hand in expectance. I was at that awkward age when teeth tend to stand out with metal bramble wood encasing them. The cute stage had left, and puberty had caused mood swings to my mother's dismay. I started to get annoyed in the length of the trip out to Detroit and could not understand why mom and dad had to stay for so long organizing Aunt Sylvia's large home. It was only later that I understood once again, how my parents love for people was not in word but also in action. My Aunty was a saver. I say that because she held on to letters, bills, and mostly everything she could. I think her heart never could fully heal. She missed her husband so badly it caused a reaction in her to hold onto things. Perhaps it was because she could hold onto things, people could die at any time. During our visits it became routine that we would have a cup of coffee, juice for me, and then I would get out my homework or some activity. Mom and dad would be asking with stern yet gentle persuasion, "Now do you need to keep this? What about this, the date is five years old?" After a few hours we would bundle into the car and go to a nice restaurant as her thank you for our visit. Even though her heart never mended her eyes always held a certain sparkle for me. She was not only my Grandmother substitute she was my Aunty whom I loved and adored. One of the great joys in my life was being able to place my first born daughter in Aunt Sylvia's arms and watch as a simple kiss was given for the first and last time on my visit to the U.S.A. Aunty died shortly after.

Finding Black Gold on the Emerald Isle

Chapter 2

The year my parents started legal proceedings to adopt me was a very intense year, full of racial tension in Detroit, Michigan. The Rodney King beating was not too long past. We felt the rippling effects as social services did not think it wise that a black child should be brought up by white parents. As a way of integrating some of what I was missing in black culture, I was made to attend an all black junior high school. It was one of the worse years of my life, as I faced enormous rejection on all fronts from the staff to the pupils. Whatever the reasons, not being able to use the slang language along with multiple other reasons, the year was one were I was constantly bullied. I fell into a teenage depression of sorts.

In my childhood years, I grew up considering myself to be the cute black kid with the pretty smile and charmingly joyful exterior. I never thought that a reuniting with people of my own race would do anything but confirm my thinking. I assumed that black people would welcome me with open arms as one of their lost joyful little girls needing assurance and a cultural nod of approval. I was wrong.

The door opened to the school year and my ideal reunion with the race I had never known, shattered, like an expensive glass dropping to the floor. The year was filled with pain and rejection. From the teaching staff to the pupils, I was made to feel like an outsider peering in with my hands cupped around my face. On the night of a special program, some of my classmates peered out the curtain and whispered these words: "Oooo, who are those white people out there?" Wanting to run away, I knew they were talking about my parents. The abyss between black and white was not to be bridged in that environment.

I find it intriguing the way life experiences tend to leave roots down deep in us to form and shape our person.

Over the next few years into my teenage life, I attended another private school. It was mostly Caucasian and I went back to being the cute black girl who laughed loudly and was friendly with most. I assumed the role again, like putting on mittens on a cold winter day. It fitted nicely.

Chapter 3

Most Americans I meet wanted to go to Ireland at some point in their life. I smile remembering how many times I heard Americans claim, "Oh yeah, I am Irish!"

When interning in the great State of Texas, I met a guy with charm and the cutest accent I had ever heard. I was his. Our stereotypes and assumptions braided together to make a sing-song young love romance. When our internship came to a close, the dream and adventure became even more of a reality when I made my first visit to Northern Ireland. I still remember the plane flying over and coming in for a landing in Dublin. The green grass, green everywhere, was dashingly glorious. The people were even more enchanting than the land. I came and I left in a whirlwind of young vision. Fresh dreams--ready to adventure across the world without understanding the pressures of international romance.

The reality started to sink in as we planned our small but intensely spiritual picturesque wedding in my home state of Michigan. We were excited to have friends flying in from many different states, Canada and N. Ireland. Our apartment was prepared to move into, honeymoon booked in Niagara Falls, and a life plan unfolding. My Love was arriving days before the wedding. With my parents and his best man in tow, we went to pick him up from the airport. Excited was not adequate to describe my feelings. People started flooding out of the arrival gate. I waited. It honestly felt like hours went by; he never came out. Once again the feeling of reality crashing my romantic idea of the way things should be washed over every fiber of my being. He was not allowed to enter the USA due to a misunderstanding of the visa issued. He was deported back to N. Ireland, and our wedding was cancelled. Devastation crowded in on our young love. Within weeks, I was on a plane to N. Ireland with a new adventure quickly carved into previous plans. A small wedding with very few people that I knew took place. My parents and my longtime mentor and Pastor came to take part in marrying me to my Irish Gent. The marriage papers were signed.

Sadly, like most dreamed about adventures where reality does not have a space, our marriage began to fall apart and was over in four short years. Once again that feeling of life choices crashing in on my Anne of Green Gables and Doris Day ideals ensued.

The beauty of experiencing an organically grown family by choice not blood, colored my decision to stay in Northern Ireland after the divorce. My first reaction of course was to run home and be with my parents. After pondering I realized how important it would be for my children to have both parents in the same country. If I had a penny for every time I have been asked,"Why on earth are you in this country? Why did you stay?" There are so many other personal reasons, but one, is the look on my mother and father-in-laws face when they held their first grandchild, they fell in love immediately. My own parents have a unique love for my children in a way that words do not give justice, but they also have many grandchildren that they love and cherish.

When I moved to Northern Ireland I experienced many "firsts," being a wife, homemaker, daughter and sister-in-law, and foreigner. I was in enormous culture shock and trying to understand how this western country could be so tremendously different to home.

My memories are fresh of my husband's parents. The first observation of my Father-in-law was the twinkle in his eye. I quickly noticed the amusement he found in his own sense of humor. I have not met a person, as of yet, that has thoroughly enjoyed his own joke before it finished rolling off his tongue. I concluded this to be why he wears the proof of this amusement in smile lines around his eyes. The twinkle in his eye is enough to make anyone grin. Upon learning the difference in the British Pound to the U.S. Dollar in my arrival, my father-in-law was explaining how USA cents are the N. Irish pence and also we had the dollar but they have the pollar. It was only after asking a shop assistant how many pollars an item was that I knew his joke had fooled me.

My Mother-in-law is a generous, modern and yet classy sort of woman. She has an underlining strength that causes my curiosity to speculate how one arrives at that destination. I remember the day she taught me to make the famous Irish stew. For some reason, I won't forget the day because it was special making the country feel a bit more like home. One of the big things I noticed was the way my Mother-in-law dressed and presented herself. She always looked well and nicely put together. I quickly knew that I could ask her anything and was free to speak with her at ease.

I have not met a couple who are such great friends and truly enjoy each others' company while still fancying each other as my in laws. What a lovely heritage to pass down.

Divorce can be messy and families are torn in two, each family taking sides. My In-Laws conducted themselves with such grace and respect for their son and me that it would teach some of the highest paid family mediators a lesson. They have been such wonderful grandparents to our children from the moment they held them in their arms.

Chapter 4

Here I was a foreigner in Northern Ireland with two babies, living in a little city just outside Belfast. I had a church family that kept me sane. My in-laws were most helpful with my toddlers. Nevertheless soon it began--a life of survival that forced me to grow up and become a woman. Finding it hard to accept the day-to-day difficulties of being a single mother, I struggled to accept responsibility. I found that my life was turning out very differently than my silly, little girl naiveties because of my choices and actual reality. I have always struggled with being a realistic person, the whimsical dreamer. As reality swept in like a bold gust of wind, sometimes my days stood still.

Money was very tight and I had to pick and choose my luxuries. Hair. On arrival in this country, I found out quickly that I could not go to the local supermarket and buy hair products that cater to my type of hair like I could in the USA. Black peoples' hair and white peoples' hair are completely different; let's be honest and to the point! After much trepidation, I found an African lady who owned a salon in Belfast. Since she was the only salon owner in the country that I had found to style my hair, I decided to get dreadlocks. At the beginning of my marriage it was nice, but dreadlocks are permanent and when boredom descended, I had to cut them out. The result got very expensive, to my husbands' dismay and lack of understanding of my hair structure. At that point, I went and got it chemically straightened and styled at one of the two salons catering to African American type hair. Then, when I was no longer married and struggling financially, I started to think of a cheaper solution.

One summer, on a visit home to Michigan, I was looking online and began to research some hair ideas. It seemed that Beyonce and Tyra Banks wigs were all the rage in the good ole USA. They were not that expensive in comparison to trips to the hairdressers, so I decided to invest my dollars in a wig. It arrived and I enjoyed the way the hair flung about when I moved. It was almost like my little girl dream of being Anne of Green Gables with the long flowing hair. In my eyes I was successful and I was hooked. After I returned to Northern Ireland, I thought it practical to shave off my own hair and just wear wigs. I went back to church with my wonderfully favorite people in the country. The reaction to "my hair" was charismatic. I was pleased even though it had not really dawned on me that it was not actually my hair.

The day came when my little girls who had heads full of shiny, bouncy curls said, "Mum when can I wear straight hair?" The question hit me like a ton of bricks. In my eyes, my girls could not be more perfect. Even though they each had different hair structure, it was beyond beauty in each and every curl. Although not intentionally, I was feeding them the message that my own hair was not good hair. Thus began another chapter in my hair journey. I threw away the wigs and let my hair grow as God intended it to grow.

Chapter 5

~ I felt like a deer running along side a stunning herd of white antelope ~

After a year or so of being on my own, I heard through mutual church friends of another African American woman living in my city. Eventually we met and hit it off immediately; what a wonderful friend I found in her.

I have always been smiley and bubbly and made friends easily, minus the one horrid school year. Therefore, when Shana came along, I was not lacking wonderful people in my life to hold my hand through tough times and laugh with me in happy ones. However, I could never have anticipated the impact this woman would have on me.

As time went by, I started to notice a few more black people in the city. My girls and I lived close to the army barracks where I met a few African families who were serving in the Army. Before long I made friends with a lovely girl from Malawi who attended my church.

All of these friendships, amidst my amazing family in the Northern Irish community, were starting to make me examine how I fitted into my skin and what my race actually meant to me.

One early summer day, I was at the train station with my African American friend Shana. We were looking forward to a day in the big city of Belfast. She had stepped away for a moment when a very handsome black man approached me and politely introduced himself. My heart started racing and sweaty palms followed. He said that he had noticed me on previous occasions and had not taken the opportunity to say hello. He was in the British Army but originally from Kenya. Summer romance chased me like a little puppy nipping at my heels. As summer ended, so did my first relationship with a black man when he had to move away to England to pursue a new career.

I saw myself in a new light after that. My being was stirred and my thoughts unfolded on paper.

I will be in your debt for years into the bright of my future.

As the chains of familiar history of one, maybe two mothers up the tree of their family, my girls will wonder how Mommy got free.

While not all your doing, all glory to Him in the heavens, I pause and say thank you for the freedom you brought me and my generations.

In your organic black swagger and approving look on my existence, I am curious to find out if the black man when sitting back in his old age realizes just how much we needed his nod of "It's ok my dear; go ahead and soar my dear."

Not sure if it was your firm grip around my waist or the tone of your nonjudgmental laugh that slipped in the key that opened the door on the cage to my beauty.

You are an old soul.

Whatever strong power you possessed to unlock the door and set my drive to flight, don't lose it please. My daughters and their daughters will thank you as the wings of theirs are formed watching me soar. The first in my mothers line, her battered cage of addictions lined with needles and judgmental laughter, the men in her surroundings chose to pull at her with their hands ripping at her body not fully developed, with her wings not given the chance to heal and form strength. The gate she locked it from inside. Quick now hide; quick now hide.... With her drug of choice, many needles cut the key to perfection.

Yet I am free. Now I will fly. I will love, and I will die. Yes, I am free and I will fly. I will love, and I will die; but there will be a trail of breathtaking heart stopping beauty cut into keys of great perfection for my daughters and their daughters to come.

You are an old soul and a wise soul.

I thank my God for you and your kingly robes.

Chapter 6

Northern Ireland maintains the reputation of having some of the friendliest people on earth. On a typical day for me and my little ones, we would walk into town. Like the tiny town where I used to spend my summers in Michigan's Upper Peninsula, the people would usually say hello, give a wee head nod and make a wee comment on the weather. Without fail, a walk into town would contain a good few long glances, comments on the girls' curls, and possible requests to touch our hair. My hair had grown out and I had become more confident in myself as a strong adult woman of color. Now I was also more experienced in taking care of and styling my hair and the girls' hair. This confidence attracted even more attention. Some of the comments I have received over the years have made me smile and giggle. Others have annoyed me thoroughly. "How do you get your hair to stay like that? Lots of hairspray?" One experience I won't forget in a hurry was two sales girls who came to the door. I answered, preparing myself for the sales pitch. Instead, the first words from the girl's mouth were, "Oh class, look at your hair! Can I touch it? How does it get like that?" I thought for a moment; if I was not a curvy, black female with natural hair, but a skinny, blonde female with downward flowing tresses, you wouldn't dare ask such an invasive question. Of course my response was no. Afterwards, I giggled at the ridiculousness of that situation.

Northern Ireland contains a rich and vibrant history, but I find it so intriguing that its citizens don't question their identity as to race and heritage. I was shopping in Belfast with my best friend who has a E in her name, who had come for a visit from the States. As usual, we were asked for how long were we visiting and how we enjoyed the country so far. My friend answered, "Oh, she [meaning me] is from here; I am visiting from the States."

The girl behind the counter was clearly not amused at the statement of a black girl ever "being from here." Nearly everyone born here is Northern Irish, possibly having family roots from the south of Ireland, but that's it. I had grown up living in the United States, and no matter the color of a person's skin, or the type of language/accent they had, if they said they came "from the States," it was not really up for debate in my mind. Many ethnic diversities make up my home country, so it is odd to me to fathom the thought of knowing who the foreigners were just by a glance. It must be quite a safe feeling, to know who is who. Being an artist and romantic at heart, I am not sure which I would prefer. Would I prefer the camaraderie of being part of the richly similar heritage majority or the unique feeling of eclectic flavorful diversity?

Another part of the history of this beautiful land has to

do with the Troubles this country has faced over the years. The height of these Troubles started in the late sixties between the Nationalist and Unionist Parties, the first mostly considering themselves to be British Protestants and the latter, Irish and Roman Catholic. This led to nearly three decades of violence. As the roots of this conflict go so deep and so far back, I do not think I will ever grasp the pain each group has endured.

I remember not long after my first arrival to the country, I was aboard a ferry with my husband to Scotland when I saw a young boy must have been only about eleven years old, lighting a cigarette outside in the corner. In my home country adults believe that if a youth is doing something inappropriate, adults tend to comment. I was about to say, "Hey kid, you should not be smoking that. How old are you?" My husband could see me about to approach him and stopped me quickly, saying," Do not say anything! You don't know his family, his dad could be in the paramilitary." That day, I began to realize how different the culture was and how much I yet had to learn about life in Northern Ireland.

Chapter 7

Recently I attended a worship conference put on by an African church in Belfast. It was oddly similar to some churches back home in the States. I enjoyed worshipping God in the Gospel type setting. It felt homey. The people welcomed my daughters and me like family and that was a nice feeling.

After that enjoyable African concert experience, the importance of culture penetrated my consciousness. What type of cultural immersion and exposure did I want for my little girls? Their confusion and my surprise and embarrassment were evident when my eldest daughter first met my friend Shana. She asked her: "Why do you have the same color face as my Mommy?"

This experience made me consider that it would take more than one black friend in the city to immerse my daughters in the flavorful cultural experience I wanted for them. This prompted my decision to start attending the African church once a month with my girls, and to get involved with some great ethnic diversity networking as well. Since then I have seen a slight shift in my little girls' thinking and my own. The road ahead is still long, but it's worth every effort. I am enamored with dipping my toes into the pond of African culture. There is a kinship in our blood that tells a story. Curiosity begs me to investigate its origins. I have made some beautiful friends along this journey so far.

I love a quote I heard on the documentary,"The Black Power Mixtape 1967-1975:" "America is a young dumb country and it needs all kinds of help. America is a dumb puppy with big teeth that bite and hurt. And we take care of America. We hold America to our bosom; we feed America, we make love to America. There wouldn't be an America if it wasn't for black people. So you have some dedicated black Americans who will die a million deaths to save America. And this is home for us. We don't know really about Africa. We talk it in a romantic sense, but America is it. And so, America is always going to be okay as long as black people don't totally lose their mind, cause we'll pick up the pieces and turn it into a new dance." — Abiodun Oyewole

Sad but true some of my limited knowledge about Africa is based on watching the series of movies called *Roots*.

Excitement draws me to create my own beginnings. I don't really know my birth Mother and never met my birth Father. I know, despite the weakness my birth mother showed, I come from a strong bloodline. I have to. By God's grace I am here and still standing.

Chapter 8

Curvy Queen.

I have always been curvaceously Rubenesque. Growing up at home, my Mother always strived for healthy living. She cooked in a wholesome manner including lots of good nutritious food. Since my parents were older when I came to live with them, they always fought hard to maintain a healthy physique. Now that I am an adult, I can see, how they looked into my future and secured healthy habits so they would be around to raise me into adulthood. When I was four months old, I came to live with my fifty year old mother and father. My dad always joked that mom would make him walk a couple miles before he got his breakfast. It was mostly true. They walked miles and enjoyed riding bicycles together. The story after story I could tell about our family adventures. My parents did not feel the need to conform to the way other families chose to do things.

Dad and mom were quite happy creating an environment based on the Word of God and their own unique adventuresome souls. I remember being in the family sailboat very far out on Lake Michigan in the Upper Peninsula. The wind started to pickup and waves began to form; my memory recalls that I was about four or five years old. Dad was scrambling   around the boat trying to get control of the sail and mom had her hand on the rudder. I knew something was going very wrong. After not too long, but seeming like years, our boat capsized! We all had life jackets on but I remember thinking we were going to die. The boat even hit dad on the head; mom had a tight hold of me and tried to cling onto the boat. The water was freezing and the look in my parents' eyes was not good. Mom was praying. Thankfully someone had seen the accident from their lakeshore cottage and called the much needed rescue team. We were brought back to shore, shaken but safe. We were glad to feel the sand beneath our feet. That was one of my more theatrical childhood adventures! We did not stop sailing. Never allowed to be stuck in fear, we kept sailing. My parents were not people whose actions were based on fear or if so, they certainly would not have adopted a little black girl in amidst the racist winds of our times.

My dad was a legend. He always said that God gave him the "gift of helps," and he was forever helping people. He could fix anything. I mean anything! He was a carpenter, just like Jesus. What I will always appreciate most about my daddy is his continuous encouragement to me: "Letta, I truly believe you can do anything, ANYTHING you set your mind to do." He would always say, "From the moment you came into our lives, I knew God had a big plan for your life!"

I have always had the expectation that things would not

be "normal" for me. The heart inside me beats romance; the blood coursing through my veins rivers adventure and my oxygen is Grace Himself.

Chapter 9

This beautiful country of Northern Ireland, even in its weakness, breathes beauty. The green is so vividly green because of the frequently visiting rain. Sometimes, just when you feel the rain is the country crying out from years of pain through each raindrop, you speak to a local person and that thought is changed. The people are kind to a certain degree of ease and comfort. Once you understand it is the lens we all see through, and that it could be seen like a deer in a herd of white antelope, then it's all ok. We are all just people. People living everyday where we make our homes.

This spot on earth will always have a place in my heart.

In my life up to date, I have had a few high swells of love and undercurrents of sad endings.

I met a beautiful man and what a swell of love that was!

We met and the experience of love that occurred will not soon be forgotten.

Not only was he gorgeous and dark, like the darkest of chocolate, but he spoke French as his first language. His faith was unlike other people I have met: strong and secure in the God we both served, I admired him from the start. His eyes were set back deep in his search yet assurance of God although they sometimes contained a hollowness--a lack in the experience of lasting love.

The first day I met him, he serenaded me in a park. The relationship was painted with the most beautiful colors and the most romantic high notes that could be sung. Sadly, it was not to be, and we parted ways.

I was taken aback at the thought of losing another great love and started to reflect on whether something was wrong with me. I thought of what I might have done better and what more I could have done. Then I realized, no, I did what I could and I had to remain true to myself. The wisdom of maturity was such a beautiful gift compared to times past. What a gift, to not throw stones of accusations and blame at each other.

The need for attention raised its head. The idea of lonely days mixed with the unknown future proved to be what I thought I could not bear. I thought these thoughts.

Why do we take caution with measuring out faith? Why do I sometimes tip toe in trepidation like my way is somehow better than His? I have decided, uncomfortable as it is I will get out my camera and take a creative shot of these walls. The smell is fiercely putrid but I want to remember the detail, and the smell of bile. Because it will not be forever. The fish that swallowed me has not disabled my destiny. In fact the very residence inside this creature may have superseded the tip toe pace of the past, propelling me forward into a new and brighter place.

Chapter 10

From the day the Kenyan soldier stopped me, he had awakened a part to my womanhood I had not known to exist.

While thankful that I became aware of part of my being that was worthy of pursuit it also had led me to make one of the worst decisions of my life.

A decision wherein I chose to enter a room setting my morals to the side and trading my purity for a hand to hold. I became addicted to the attention of handsome men who seemed to adore me. The trade, and the sacrifice in those choices proved costly. Seeing it as an empowerment of my womanhood when it was really a loss of my Queenship. The very perfume of attraction was my heart for God, yet I ended in the stench of thinking I was in control of my future.

I entered the room and the mirror stood in front of me reflecting a puzzle I was trying to piece together in my mind. After applying makeup that improved myself and knowing it would impress the target of my audience, I smiled. The departure of the Kenyan long past, the suiters still came. Men who seemed ready and willing to give me the attention that I craved.

Throughout my life I recognized the hand of God at work. I knew that the compass of compromise only lead to a life without peace. Addicted to the attention of men who were ready to "love" me as long as I held tight to the compass kept me in a room of carnival mirrors.

The mirror stood in front of me reflecting a Queen wearing no shoes. I saw the door to exit but the thought of returning to the days of walking with my head held down frightened me. Could I trust God enough to go backwards returning to the days of wearing invisible as my attire and hoping that a good man was yet to come? I was a divorced mother of two little girls. What could I really offer? The mirror reflected an overweight tired Mother, who had to tighten her grip on the compass in order to be seen.

Little did I know that behind the scenes, and the room full of mirrors something was at work. The God I had known as a little girl was real. The angel that I had seen in my room long ago was real and surrounded by countless others like him.

It was the day that I was thrown overboard that ushered me out of the room of mirrors. A few friends and leaders took me by the hand and much to my dismay tossed me over the boat and into the sea. It was freezing and I could not seem to catch my breath. My body went into shock as the icy waves splashed over me. The whale of rejection and abandonment swallowed me whole again. I felt that he had been pursuing me since I came outside the womb of my mother.

I started to realize that part of my story on this Emerald Isle was finding out who I really am.

I look in the mirror and see a blur. I often think how simple it would be if I could just see my reflection. Instead, I see myself covered in a shawl of bad decisions, a hat of smiles and the heartbeat of motherhood.

I wish to see the part of me that says, "Don't stay and fight for me." Although the deeper I look, the more I understand it is I who has to fight. No one can win my battles for me. God aids and equips and there is a battle that is all ready won. I need to get on my hard hat, light the carbide lamp, and look into the caves of my being to find that which is gold.

There are those people that seem to walk above the clouds dipping their toes in the rain clouds as if it were a mere pond. The thoughts of ones such as these seem so delightful. Most assuredly and even more delightful when the thoughts are to do with me. One such person I consider friend and sister, shared her plumply ripe thought with me. This simple idea of her match-making inspired my daydreams for days-- daydreams which played the first song in the soundtrack sung by three young sisters, singing and dancing to the hope of Yenta making a good match. In their childhood frivolity, they feared that a man existed worthy of their hearts. My friend had simply mentioned a man she thought would go well with me. Yet the man she named seemed like he would have walked above the clouds with her. The idea that I could possibly take his hand and be lifted above the clouds sent butterflies a flutter in my stomach. The very thought, encircled in a hope of viewing my worth from a different angle, was enticing. The men I had been dating as of late seemed to be side tracked by street sweeping. The choice made to busy themselves with the fetching of once in a while fancies whilst living, just living. These men dawned no ladder with any desire to mine or climb. Inside of me is an enormous need to mine the cave of life, to find the black gold. A need to climb above the clouds experiencing rain from the opposite side. I long to see what my mother and father believed would come to pass. My life was to mean something more. I was saved from the drug rut for a reason. Digging and dreaming, my friend nudged me to dig deeper still.

Chapter 11

Digging and dreaming

I awoke before dawn. Preparing to leave before first light was the goal I had successfully reached. Backpack filled with tools for the job, the heaviness did not outweigh the resplendent joy on the hunt for treasure. Having in the past been waylaid on a few recent mornings, I was determined to continue the hunt. The only seemingly brightness that guided my journey was the most enchanting color of green ever to be in existence. This shade of green I am convinced was only found in one place on earth, the Emerald Isle. Quickening my pace, as I could see the sun was thinking of showing his face, I decided to jog. After about five minutes, the load was too heavy and I resumed a slower pace. Then I saw the mouth of the cave. I knew then I had beat the sun and it did not make an iota of difference as I would be working in the darkest absence of light anyway. I lit the carbide lamp and set all the necessary tools in a row. I gripped the mining pick, lifted it, eyeing just where it was to land and CHIP! It landed with precision. Stones flew out and dust clouded around me, filling my nostrils and lungs swift and quick.

The day I thought I had Body Dysmorphic Disorder shot up from the smoke and I knew that was my next job to work through, to find what I had come to find.

I saw my reflection in the shop window and gasped inside my mouth. Then a yelp caught in my throat for a second as I picked up the pace to see the next window to glance in. AGAIN, there it was. Who was she? How did the enormous person in that reflection dare leave and enter the public? How could she be surprised at the disgust he felt for her? She could almost taste the dismay, disgust and regret like she threw it all up in her mouth. That person reflecting was surely undeserving of love. She had ruined everything and deserved the consequences that came in the months following. Love had walked out the door, leaving her alone once again. The feeling was so familiar. I knitted a shawl in the reality of its being and wrapped it tightly around my shoulders to fend off the draft of its' absence. At home alone with no adult interaction, I poured out a glass of wine to help solve the overwhelming acceptance of fault. Another glass confirmed it. I had done this to myself with my breaking of the law and unsuccessful attempt at chiseling out someone different. Firstly, I should have paid more attention to respect. Respect for him and respect for myself. I screwed that up and just kept on that road. How utterly disappointing it all turned out to be. If it had not been for the two stars that fell from heaven itself sleeping in their little beds, I am sure my head would have sunk into the nearest ocean. To breathe everyday was hard, to take one step, even harder. No one can understand how this tasted to me. To me, yet who was I? Who was I really? I could not see clearly anymore. The reflection I saw was utter painful words wrapped in failing hope.

All of a sudden I tasted blood! The mining pick had flung a piece of debris at my mouth and my lip had begun to bleed. I licked it away and kept digging. I felt I was close to breaking into a new level of rock.

Just as red as the blood on my mouth, it was his red sports car slowing down and giving a bold honk that caused me to glance away from the disappointing reflection of who I thought I was. I looked at him without really looking and used my concentration to take the next step in front of me. Hoping that I could finish the day was a triumph in itself.

A few weeks later, I came face to face with someone who resembled the man in the car. Yes, it was the Kenyan solider in the British Army. He was the first to wake me up out of the dysmorphic trance that had me in lockdown. It was his eyes. When I looked into them, I saw the opposite of what the shop window had told me. Those eyes screamed, you are alive and your heart beats beauty, your veins pump exquisite royalty. I never wanted to look away. It was as if I could swim in the pool of reflection, as if hope was alive and well in that reflection. I came close to giving up all I had to lock eyes with him and make him promise to never look away. Humanity fails us; in all its divinity, it fails. He left. I ran and grabbed my shawl and lightly held it in my hands. The breeze had turned warm so I did not need to wear it just yet.

I decided to remember what I had seen in his eyes. They did not lie. I put on lipstick, pulled a floaty dress over my head and took another step.

Hours passed and my arms throbbed with the swing of the pick. I thought to sit down would be best for a moment. Just as I sat, wet began to seep through my clothes, I thought I had sat in a puddle of water, then I realized I was covered in sweat. I took the carbide lamp and shuffled to the entry of the cave. Peering through nearly closed eyelids, the sun hurt my eyes. The green on every hill surrounding also reflected such brightness, and I thought to return inside. It was the enticing breeze that caressed my cheek and cleared my smoky lungs, persuading me to stay a few minutes longer. I assessed the work that needed still to come before the day was through. I knew I had broke through another level of stone and was closer to the treasure, yet I did not know how to measure just how many more levels of digging I would have to do.

Daunting, yet seducing, the wonder the cave held was intoxicating. I remembered that for now no one else knew about this cave. I had stumbled upon it myself one day. Having had dreams about it for years and seeing myself finding the treasure it contained, I knew this was part of my destiny. To find this treasure, I was enamored with the quest. All the gumption it took to pick up that mining pick once more filled my body. Back to the work, enthralled with the dreams of long gone past.

Smoke once again filled the small corner where I had been working and through it I saw a shimmer. Dropping the pick with a thud that echoed throughout the cave, I dramatically clawed off my gloves and dug my fingers into the debris and stone. Grasping the small stone, I brought it over to the carbide lamp for closer examination. Was this it? Was this the gold, the treasure that I was looking for? I held it close as I began to feel my fingertips scratched and bleeding. I spit on the rock and shined it on my coat. YES, it was shining a tiny shimmer yet it was most definitely my first find. Tiny as that rock was, the adrenaline that surged and drove me back to exactly where I found it caused me to work harder still. What if that rock had a family down there? A family of treasure. The smoke was thicker still and I hunted like a woman possessed.

Through the smoke out waddled a duck. I kid you not. A duck not very big at all, covered and smothered in all sorts of black debris and dirt from the cave. In the midst of blinking my eyes a few times out of sheer confusion, it was her sickly quack that confirmed its actual existence. As she approached me quickly, all a fuddled like, she was in a hurry to escape something, I realized just how ugly she was. The ugly duck was not just covered in black smoke and dirt, her feathers were actually a dark and dirty brownish black. I became quickly annoyed and angered that she was distracting me from the purpose and obsessive desire to reach my goal. The silly little thing came right between my feet and sat down.

I have never been a fan of creatures with wings, so I sort of froze, not knowing what to do. I suddenly wished my friend, who was the fan of these horrid creatures was here to advise. I stared closer at this little thing and thought, my goodness, it's so awful looking. I thought whoever was in pursuit of it must surely be desperate! Before the thought had cleared my mind, out from the smoke came two little ducklings! I could hardly believe my eyes, they were tiny. They tried to climb over little stones in just as much a hurry as their mother seemed to be. The only problem was, their little webbed feet could not coordinate with their rush. Unlike their mother, they were such little beauties. I quickly went over, the fear of winged creatures abandoned and I scooped them up in my hands. Flustered and flapping, they seemed to calm down once the mother gave another quack. Out of the mouth of the cave we came and into the sunlight we went.

I followed the Momma duck to a close pond and she waddled in, whilst I did not want to let the babies go. They were so delightfully cute in their miniature everything. As dirty duck got in the water, I saw her flap and thrash about causing her to lift her wings and dip her head into the water. She was having a bath and I almost wanted to giggle. The transformation that took place surprised me fully. She was not ugly. She was the most beautiful shade of brown with flecks of blue and green in her feathers. I actually saw what appeared to be gold flecks on her head. I was flabbergasted at the transformation of this little bird and reluctantly placed the little ducklings in the water to be with their mother. I was observant in watching them swim with precision beyond their size. They copied mother duck in bathing themselves and transformed from adorable little ducklings to keenly golden little navy seal beauties. Swimming in circles it was as if they were dancing like a bunch of old ladies showing off their synchronized moves. With regal pride, the Mother led the two ducklings down the pond and just as the last view of them escaped me, I saw a fox emerge on the green hill. He too was seeing the last view of them swim past. A quick vision of what could have been, played through my mind as I sighed a sigh full of grateful relief that I may have helped them escape. What an afternoon this was, what a distraction pleasantly surprising, though the reality of the work I had to accomplish still sunk in my stomach. I knew the day of work was nearly past and yet so much still I had to do. Jogging back to the opening, I was glad I had all the sharp tools at my side since who knew just what the cave held in residence beside treasure, ducks and foxes. Dear me!

Chapter 12

Even though my body was aching and exhausted as it neared dinner time, I knew I wanted at least one more hour of work. I had an inkling so much more was in the area where I had found the first bit of gold. Settling on my knees and choosing to use the finer picks and hammers, I saw only black. I began to hum a tune, unsure of where I heard it, yet its familiarity got me thinking. Was it in a dream? Not sure, just as my thoughts searched my memory I saw a glint of something. Yes, there it was! Gloves off and a quick lick of the fingers to get the dirt off, and yes it was only slightly bigger than the small pebble before, but it was there. I held it up close to my face as my heart beat faster. This had to be a sign that something bigger was close. This could be it, my big break. Finding this could turn my life completely around not having to worry as much about finances as I did everyday.

Just as hope was rising like white-capped waves in the Irish Sea, I heard it. Oh the sound had become as familiar as the full moon on a clear night or footsteps of a close friend. Rain was the way the green shone its best. I heard it start to pound and echo over the cave walls. Some even ran down the walls as if it was petting it, like a cat purring on its back. I was so excited to dig, I ignored it even though I knew the wisest option would be to pack up and start again in the morning.

I began to dig in the same place straining my eyes to see any more shimmer. Then I heard an unwanted sound. It was possibly an animal, another fox? Dropping the little tool, I grabbed the big hammer and looked out the mouth of the cave. I thought no one knew I was here. Panic set in as I thought whoever it was would want to steal my treasure. I couldn't afford that! I bent down and turned down the carbide lamp with caution as I knew I would not even be able to see my hands in front of me. Using my ears as my eyes, I was as quiet as I could possibly be. Holding my breath, I heard the person approaching the mouth of the cave.

It was then fear and confusion set in. My heart began to slow. Was what I was hearing correct? I strained to hear the muffled sound. Yes, it was coming from whomever this was approaching, the tune I had been previously humming. It was a woman singing the words, between sniffles and grunted moans. "Little star, Little star, there you are in my arms..." I was certain now that the tears took over the song in a sad crescendo and I could not hear any more movement.

As much as I could not afford to be found with my treasure and I knew I looked a mess, the idea she could be hurt took over. I turned the carbide lamp up and realized that she was closer than I thought. We both jumped back as we startled each other in proximity. I took in the sight before me and my heart slowed even more still. The lady was dark skinned like myself and looked in far worse shape than I. She did not look a mess from hard work but more from hard living. I assumed she was without a home and occupying rough times as her bedfellow. Her frame was painfully frail and it looked like some of her hair was missing. Her front tooth was gone and hands smeared with something I did not care to guess at. Through the mess, her eyes were sorely hypnotic; she was reciting a poem from a long distant memory. All of a sudden she seemed as if to get dizzy and I stepped in to catch her from falling like a feather. As swift as a little mouse, she flinched back as if I was going to harm her. I said, "Oh, I thought you were going to fall! I won't hurt you." When she spoke, it was I that felt dizzy at the sound of her voice. "No, I am fine, thank you."

I had heard that voice before but could not remember where. I did not recognize her and longed for the brightness of day to see her clearly. Thinking again of my treasure, I decided to divert her away from my workplace. I spoke very softly and said," There is a river not far from here. Would you like me to show you? I can bring some food if you're hungry at all."

"Oh honey, are you sure?" she replied in a polite mother-like way.

"I would be delighted to share some food with you. I packed far too much anyway!" I said with a cute smile.

Guilt hovered the back of my head like a hangover from

a night's frolics. I knew I was being selfish, only wanting her away from my cave even though her state was no real threat. I grabbed my coat and lunch pail and we headed away from the cave.

"So what brings you out here on this awful rainy day?" I ventured. She muttered and murmured an answer and I took from that she either did not want to answer or she had none. We walked on in an uncomfortable silence. I was thinking how rare it was to get people of my color in N. Ireland at all let alone in the middle of nowhere.

I had found the cave on a hike one day, trying to clear my head of all its worry. I have never been one for great direction skills. A passion of mine is photography, so I thought a wee hike out in the trails would be great for some creative shots. It was that day I came across the caves. Being half city girl, half country, I was dually torn about peeking inside. I went with my gut and turned right around, hiked the few miles back to the city and entered the nearest coffee shop. I got out my phone and googled the location. In the weeks that followed, I researched the caves and read the stories and history behind them. Reading that gold had been rumored in thereabouts, the anchor was tossed into the sea of my adventure. I would hunt the treasure. I would find that black gold!

"What food is it?"

Hearing the woman's voice brought me back to the

situation at hand. A bit surprised at the abruptness of the question, I replied in the same fashion without actually meaning to. "Ham and cheese sandwich and crisps. Pecan pie and coffee for dessert!"

We crouched down to sit and before my behind hit the ground she snatched the bag out of my hand and tore it open as if she had not eaten for weeks. Grunting and mumbling through bites, I just sat there awkwardly not knowing where to look. The rain tapering off, I was able to see her more clearly as the sun shone bright red in its descent.

"Honey, who taught you how to bake this pecan pie? It tastes just like my Grandma used to make."

"My Mother taught me," I replied quickly, surprised that she even had a Grandma. She was such an eerie sight; it seemed like she had not another soul in the world.

As she polished off the first flask capful of coffee, she slightly choked on the second cup, reaching it over to me.

"Baby I'm sorry, I am so rude, would you like this one?"

It was at that point annoyance set in. Who was she to offer it to me like she was doing ME a favor? Also what was with the Baby, and Honey? She looked the same age as me, in fact slightly younger. I assumed it was her harsh lifestyle choices that made her face look old beyond its years.

"No, you have it, its fine." I said, as my own belly growled, not used to being neglected for more than a morning and afternoon, let alone all day. I sensed that she did not pick up on the strained tone in my voice, as she smiled and drank it straight down.

She tossed over the lunch pail and shuffled around so that she could reach her back pocket and got out something in a wadded crumple. Uncomfortably I watched as she boldly rolled up what I was certain to be a marijuana joint. Eyes rolling in my head, I thought to myself, hmmhmmm of course she is. Thinking how I didn't have time to waste on this woman, and my good deed was done for the week, I jumped to my feet. Unbothered and not even embarrassed, she reclined puffing away happy and content.

"Well, I have to be on my way back home now." I said. "It was lovely to meet you. My name is Willetta, what's yours?"

Without even straining her neck to turn, she peered off at the sunset and said, "Baby, thank you. My name is Simone."

Once again, curious as to her referring to me as one young and less together, I decided to leave my tools behind so she would not notice my precious hidden cave. I was sure she would not as she did not even notice me leave and start the walk back into town.

Chapter 13

The ticket collector on the train placed his hand on my shoulder and gave me a gentle nudge. "This is your stop is it not? Long day?" I shyly thanked him for waking me up out of the doze I had let myself drift into. Getting off the train in the dark was not my normal routine; I preferred getting home earlier than this. Still slightly resentful about the woman who disrupted my routine, I felt too tired to care. I took the last step to my front door, unlocked it and went inside. Comfort at last; the smell of warm vanilla sugar wafted by my nose with the close of the door. Candles and beautiful scents were a need in my home; they brought calm to my senses. Tonight it was true especially. I enjoyed a mug of soup and the hottest bath my skin could stand, before allowing my bed to capture me for the night. My brain and body were wrecked; the scents tucked me into my bed.

As tired as I was, I woke at three a.m. and four a.m. tossing and turning hearing the song being sung, being hummed, "Little star. Little star." Disrupted as my sleep chose to be, the alarm on my phone sympathized with no one. I hit snooze three times and on the third remembered the importance of leaving before sunrise. Not only was the country a small one, but the town I lived in was minuscule.

Word tended to travel fast, even faster when you stood out in a crowd and had a nice chunky circle of friends. Although my circle was wide, I knew my friends had curious notions and concerns as to why they had not seen me as of late. Sleeping in instead of attending church was highly unusual for me. I loved the house of God and the family that occupied it there, but I was willing to sacrifice everything to find this treasure. I knew I must find what I was looking for or it would be an ever rotting shell that attended church and coffee with friends.

I started to dress, hardly able to lift the shirt over my head. My body was not used to such hard work, yet my core was full of determination, enough to find more gold today. The town was empty. As I walked through, it felt like an old western that my Dad used to watch. I halfway expected the doors of the pub to swing open and to see a man with cowboy hat tilted as if to point his twin barreled gun at me. But instead it was just quiet. The trains were not even running yet. Picking up the pace, I reached the trail in good time. My boots were freshly glazed in the dew from the grass. The hills stunned me with their boldly voluptuous curves every single day. Because it was not the country of my birth, I still looked at it with fresh eyes in awe and appreciation. I could hear Julie Andrews' jealousy of my witness of these beauties everyday. The sound of music was definitely here in these green hills.

Nearly reaching my destination and just beating the

sun dawning his head, my heart sank at the sight that unraveled. All of my determination and hopes for the day sank to my feet like lead and held my feet fastened to the ground. I nearly fell over. A group of people, yes right in the middle of this woods before dawn. It looked as if they were surrounding something on the ground. "Oh Jesus, please let it not be my tools and equipment!" I prayed quickly and quietly.

"God, please, please, I need this! Don't let them take my treasure!" But it was then that the people became more detailed and clear to me. I saw one middle aged man stand up slowly, zipping up his trousers. He even had a suit on. I was bewildered at the brazenness of that action. He threw down some money in the circle, then he quickly walked away looking all around him almost like he was going to be caught. What had he been doing? Then a young girl only about fourteen years old latched her arms around his waist begging him to stay and he pushed her off. The girl knelt in front of whatever they surrounded and held her head in her hands and wailed. She then quickly snatched the money the fellow had thrown down and stuffed it in her pocket.

There was also a grown woman in a nurse's uniform quickly bending down over whatever it was in the center. I saw her shaking her head as if to say, "Not again." I then saw an older black man start to kick violently what was in the circle. He took off his belt in a rage and I saw the dust fly all around the place. I began to panic, I should not be here seeing this. I did not want to get involved as I could see these people were up to no good. I started to turn around before anyone saw me and that is when I heard her. "Go ahead, just give me some more." I instantly recognized the voice. It was her. It was the black girl I had seen the day before.

I bolted back around to see everyone had gone. How could that be? They were all just there and now vanished into thin air. She was there lying in a heap. I carefully walked over in case those people lurking, hiding in the wood, were planning to jump me for whatever reason. Was this a trap? "Jesus, help me," I muttered.

As I reached Simone, I felt the tears well up in my eyes. She held a needle in her hand, whilst vomit was beside her and lay like a necklace around her chest. Her skirt was torn, legs spread apart and undergarments lying round her ankles. "Simone, Simone?" I gently said touching her face softly. I took my coat off and placed it over her legs. I went to put my knees on the ground so I could try to lift her slightly. "AGHH!" Something sharp. More needles on the ground, both broken and whole. Glass all around as well--from liquor bottles all around. How did this happen? I didn't understand how she could have stayed here all night in the cold and rain. Why wouldn't she answer? I couldn't really call the police, otherwise they would ask too many questions for which I didn't have answers.

"Simone, wake up. Are you ok? What happened last

night?"

She opened her eyes. There was a surprised look on her face; her eyes were glazed like a lake covered in ice.

"Hey baby, what are you doing here?" she said in a drunken sort of drawl. "Don't worry Honey, I'm just fine. Just had a little set back but don't worry, Momma's gonna be just fine."

With those words said, she passed out in my arms like a baby overfed on milk. I sat perplexed in the wet grass and dirt. How did she think I knew her Mother? I tried to put her words together like a thousand piece 3D puzzle. I held her in my arms for what felt like hours when in fact it was only half an hour. She seemed to come out of her heavy sleep into a lighter one, entering a nightmare of some kind. She muttered and voiced things I never wanted to hear. When she opened her eyes, I could see the sun had hit the ice and it had started to thaw in her eyes.

I dared to ask, "Simone, do you remember what happened? What did those people do to you?"

She softly began to tell me her story. "Baby, I was only young, when he first came into my room. I had to numb the pain. With my first taste I was hooked." Her story after story of heart wrenchingly, unimaginable pain, strangled my heart. She shared such intimate details and left nothing out. It was beyond bearable to listen.

I interrupted her softly and said she did not need to go

Finding Black Gold on the Emerald Isle

on unless she wanted to. Simone made an effort to sit up with no avail. I think her ribs were broken in the beating. I helped her up to a slouchy, yet uncomfortably close face to face position. She took my face into her hands; hands that felt rougher than sand paper. Close beyond comfort, I smelled the foul stench that her body produced.

I will never forget that smell as she looked me deeply in the eyes and said, "Willetta, baby, you were the strongest thing I ever did." With that, the words entered my ears and began sinking like an elevator. Stopping at each floor, they descended into my mind, soul and heart.

All at once, Simone lay down in a heap, tired and weary in the midst of drug paraphernalia and sank into the ground. Literally, it's as if she evaporated into thin air. Right before my very eyes she was gone!

I wiped and blinked my eyes over and over like I had just awakened; but I was awake and I was back in the cave, with tools all around me. I sat stunned. How could this have happened? Then the song began to play over in my mind:

"Little star, Little star lying there in my arms, Little star, Little star, how precious you are. My little one, my little baby, my one and only Little star."

Her voice was sweetly reminiscent in my subconscious. She was my mother, the one who gave birth to me. Her story flooded my thoughts; I had heard it from my adopted parents. They told me how they tried to help her get on her feet, leaving the life that would carry her to the grave. My parents had paid for her to enter rehab for a year. She had built a reputation for how beautifully she sang gospel music but she never finished the year. The call to revert back to the drugs called her name loudly over the cries of her baby. She chose them over me.

I never felt good enough; never felt wanted, because my own mother abandoned me. A dog doesn't leave its pups and that was my conclusion of her.

Yet meeting her, seeing Simone, the simple thought embraced me with the most comforting arms: *I was the strongest thing she had ever done.* In her life of bad choices, it was me, the only singular thing she was proud of. She gave me life, having given up on her own long since past. Instead of aborting me in her womb, although her circumstances screamed "Yes," she held her head up, possibly the first and last time in her life. Still addicted to the drugs she couldn't stay away from, I arrived too early at two pounds and eight ounces. But I came, I survived. I lived.

Chapter 14

I picked up the piece of gold bigger than the other two. This would be worth a lot. I dropped it into the bucket and heard its ping against the metal. Through the tears, I lifted the mining axe and started again. I would find more. There had to be more.

I worked until five p.m. Completely tired and hungry, I decided to call it a day.

I made my way to the train station and decided to go into Belfast for a bite to eat. My head was fuzzy from hunger and lack of rest. A good meal and glass of wine would surely sort out the heavy feeling of the day. My phone rang and the picture that accompanied it was a bright sun. The ringtone sang, "You are my sunshine." It was one of my dearest friends. After chatting with her for a quick minute, she was excited to meet me in Belfast for dinner and a catch up.

As I got in the taxi that would take me to my favorite Tapas restaurant in the city, my thoughts wandered over the day, but then quickly to a day not long passed. I was sitting at my kitchen table and around me a few people were giving condolences and touching my hand softly. Laurie put her hand on my shoulder and quickly put the kettle on to boil.

"Anyone for tea?" she asked the guests at the table.

"Letta, here honey, let me pour you a wee glass of wine,"Margaret gently said with tears in her eyes.

"I remember losing my Daddy..." she said.

My heart flooded with memories of my father and my mind left the room.

My dad finally lost the battle to cancer and went home to heaven to be with his favorite carpenter, Jesus. Traveling home to visit him only two weeks prior, I will always be grateful for the opportunity I had to say goodbye to him. My father asked me to play one of his favorite hymns on my violin at his funeral.

None of our family could have known that he would die on St.Patrick's Day, just two short weeks after my visit. The whirlwind of grief hardly had time to grab hold of my heart. I focused solely on my singular goal to book my flight to Michigan immediately for the funeral. I sat on the internet all night, searching through flights; I had never before experienced not being able to find a flight home until now. I noticed the airlines do something called bereavement flights and they seemed to indicate that these flights would be easier to book due to the state of grief and stress the customer had to deal with. To be honest, all I remember was a lady over the phone who was kind and offered her condolence but as far as securing a flight there appeared to be none.

My mom and I had talked over the web camera and she said to me, "Letta, we are waiting till you book your flights to confirm dates for the funeral." It was the one thing I had to do, and then I could allow grief to take its grip after I got on the plane home to Michigan. Sun dawning and birds beginning their song, it was nearly six a.m. and I was a mess; one thing and I could not seem to get it done. Later I concluded the planes were full of people traveling to and from the States and Ireland for St. Patrick celebrations. I did the only thing that came to mind. I got out my phone and called her.

Evie had been a long time friend of mine and if anyone could get me a flight, I knew she could. Although I knew it was selfish to phone her so early in the morning I did it anyway, hoping her husband and two children would not be wakened. As soon as I heard her voice the tears started to stream down my face; all I could feel was a numbness yet they flowed freely. Her voice was precious and comforting. Before anytime at all she had driven to my house ready to get the result needed.

Hours passed and my numbness grew like a wall around me. The thought that this was the one thing I had to do, *get home*. I explained to my precious daughters when they woke how Grandpa had gone to be with Jesus and that he was not in pain anymore. Though the tears flowed the numbness in me remained.

"Letta, here is the conformation; it is booked now, my friend," she said in her delicately soft mix of accents from living in many countries.

She wrapped her arms around me and the fog lifted as I looked and saw the conformation details on the laptop in front of me. Relief finally descended. I thought about how no one else could have done this with such grace and determination other than my sweet friend Evie.

Soon I was home embracing the mother that had chosen to love me and call me daughter. I was able to honor my father's request to play violin at his funeral.

I was amazed at how many people attended the funeral. So many people I remembered throughout my childhood years came wearing the cross necklace dad had made them over the years. My dad's legacy will not fully be known until we reach heaven and see in panorama how he affected so many people's lives. A little glimpse of their gratitude allowed tears to flow, and our hearts and future were inspired.

What brought me back was a little giggle from my sunshine friend Laurie. She floated about like she had ballet shoes on just to entertain everyone because she knew I had left the table, even though my body still sat there.

"Four pounds please." Oh, it was the taxi man interrupting my thoughts.

"Yes, sorry, no problem," I responded, gathering the change from my purse. I got out of the taxi and entered the restaurant. Smelling the food brought me back to the present.

Laurie and I enjoyed a bottle of wine and delicious food throughout the evening. This was bliss. We took pleasure in talking over the things of the days gone by. It was a friendship that warmed our souls. Healing and refreshing words spilled out of our mouths that had been birthed in our hearts. Full stomachs and lighter spirits, we headed back to our homes, hugging in departure.

I got into bed with my mind eased but not fully unburdened. I had to finish, I had to reach my goal.

I slept like a baby. Could it be because I had thought of those early days and come to some peace? I was coming nearer to forgiving Simone for abandoning me and decided to try to understand her life. Knowing how important forgiveness was, I decided to talk to God about my struggles.

Always feeling better after conversing with God, I decided not to rush to get ready, but to take my time this morning. I looked out the window and saw the hills in the distant skyline. Once in a while, there were days that I was still astonished to be in N. Ireland. People dream of such ventures.

I sat down at the table with my cup of coffee and thought about the night before with Laurie. She was so good for my heart. I smiled as I recalled conversations about love long lost and love very present. I thought of how we had walked through grief in losing to death people we loved.

Laurie and I shared similar admiration and enthusiasm for photography. We sharpened each other in our desire to capture people in artistic memory form. We had captured ourselves on film, nearly capturing our essence, like a firefly in a mason jar. Being myself in this country, I was used to turned necks and long glancing stares. Yet when she and I were together, our laughter seemed to shake people to their very core, causing them to question if happiness like that truly did exist.

The acknowledgment of how rich I was when it came to friendship causes my heart to be still and thank God. I truly believed that He provided me with a family of friendship in this strange country so different to my home. After time, Northern Ireland became a second home. It held people that helped me through pain I never thought I could endure.

America also had loved ones so loyal and true. One little girl with a E in her name, had been such a long time friend. The girl with an E, had the brightest of eyes. She had flown over many times just to visit me on this Emerald Isle. Good times we shared, such loyalty rare in all its fullness.

I was also aware that although rich in friendship, my life was lacking much in terms of monetary success.

When the divorce came, I felt it took me nearly five years to even stand up and take any steps at all. Whilst so common in existence in this day and age we live, divorce is a despicable tearing. That was my experience anyway, my marriage and dreams ending in such a gruesome death. I finally was able, with the help of those around me to stand.

Having two little stars to keep radiant and shooting

across the nighttime sky was an excursion in itself. How the time flew and they grew and shone so radiant; words can never do enough descriptive justice to their individual beauty.

Chapter 15

I put together the plan. If I worked hard enough and found the treasure I sought, I could confirm the security needed.

While considering how I would not want any unexpected visitors this morning at the worksite, I bent down to tie my boots. It was a bit cool so I put on my white knitted hat. Smiling at the feel and memory behind the soft stitch in each knit, I quickly finished getting ready to go.

On the train I began to heat up, my hair was usually enough without a hat. Taking the hat off, I held it in my hands, thankful that my Mom could knit so well.

My mother, Diane, was a no nonsense sort of person. I think it took until I was eighteen or nineteen years of age before she became my most treasured confidant. From my earliest recollections, she had the brightest white hair. It was beautiful. She kept it short and curly in her no nonsense sort of way. One of my favorite memories of her was her daily routine of applying her bright red lipstick. She would make an interesting and funny sort of O with her mouth. Starting with the heart shape of her top lip and ending with the bottom. It was glaringly bright red to start but then she would take one single sheet (waste not, want not) of toilet paper and blot. Blot once, blot twice and third time's the charm! The perfect look everyday. The day that routine did not take place was rare indeed.

Mom was slightly on the stern side. I can laugh at the thought presently because I have turned out similar indeed. At the time though, when mom wanted me to do something, it had better get done. If there was any hope of getting around said mission, I had to talk to my father. He was good at listening and seeing a bit more of my side. Mom and I just happened to be a bit too much alike. We were both very stubborn, yet in opposite roles, her being mom and me being daughter.

In my childhood years I neglected to notice one of the most admirable characteristics my mother holds: she is an exquisitely humble person. I am ever learning from her beautiful example. Mother would make a mistake, yes, but she would think about it. Most likely, she talked to Jesus about it, and then ask forgiveness if necessary--to Him most definitely and to whomever was involved.

Looks can be deceiving. Her outside boldness to say what she thought, without a lot of unwanted fear, could have been mistaken for a through and through sternness. My mission in life was to get past that and embrace her inner, more gentle side--the side that not every friend or companion had the privilege to see. She loved me with everything she possessed; every breath, every sigh, tear and prayer. Some days I literally knew beyond a doubt that the food in my fridge and the air in my lungs were existing because of her faithful intercessions before Abba Father. Countless hours she spent fighting in the Spirit on her knees for her children, yet even finding time to knit! As the train came to a stop, I was thick in my thoughts yet I saw him.

Chapter 16

I noticed the tall fellow who had just boarded the train.

I am one to appreciate the beauty that the human exterior can project across a room, no matter where it can radiate.

This man was over six feet tall with skin like cacao nibs. I willed my eyes to stop meeting his, but they would not obey my commands. He walked slowly past me and I realized I could release the breath I was holding. He was well dressed and held his head high. Was he one that could walk above the clouds? Oh well, just one glance at him made my morning better. About to re-enter my previous thinking, I was suddenly startled that he returned to the little table where I was sitting, asking if he may take a seat. His voice was charming, like honey dripping off a hot butter knife. I was clearly flustered and blushing, so I responded, "Of course; take a seat." Phew, my goodness, the butterflies woke up from their hibernation and decided to flutter around my insides, trying to escape.

We entered into light chitchat, discussing the weather and what we liked to do. All was grand until he mentioned his occupation. He was a rare gold dealer dealing also in small gems. I carried the little pieces of gold with me everywhere I went, but I had not wanted to get them assessed until a later date. Perhaps this could be more than a coincidence. Maybe it was fate? I think he sensed I was tangled in thought and he said, "I am sorry. Am I making you uncomfortable?" With the slightest smile and a softening of his face he continued speaking. "You are so beautiful, I just had to come and see if I could talk to you." Again, blushing deep red, I responded with a shy smile and "thank you."

I briefly mentioned that I had been looking for a gold dealer to assess a tiny stone my Grandmother had given me. I could not risk him finding out my plan or what I was doing. His expression changed and he said in a more professional tone, "My office is just near the next stop. If you have the items, I can take a look free of charge?" It was then the professionalism changed, and he gave me a coy yet amused smile."Thank you very much," I replied. "I would appreciate that. I am not sure if I have enough time this morning though."

At that moment his stop was called over the loudspeaker. I knew I would have to make a quick decision and I had only just met this man! Romantically trusting fate versus uneasy yellow caution lights fought a round in two-seconds flat. Romantic thinking won the fight. He was a dapper fellow and let me pass by him to get off first. Although feeling his eyes following me from behind, I wondered if the dapper was only just a front. He offered nicely to take one of my three bags but I was stubborn and said, "No that's fine, but thanks."

As we walked into a small dark office full of antique, quirky wee items, dust was everywhere and it smelled musty. I thought I heard voices coming from the back, almost like a meeting going on without him. "Are you sure you have time to take a look now?" I asked, wondering if he was missing out on something important, just to be kind. He shook his head yes. "There is no better company for me this morning." Coy charm must have been his expertise. He was gorgeous, perhaps the most handsome man I had ever come in contact with. He excused himself to go get the appropriate machine to sufficiently inspect the nugget.

In his absence the butterflies died, one by one, and began to fall to the bottom of my stomach like heavy weighted dumbbells. Was this a daft idea? Was I too trusting? Wait, I am a good judge of character. Surely he was just a kind and generous person. He came back with a small gem microscope. "Before we get started, how about an espresso?" he asked. A bit awkward, I responded some sort of silly, "Yea, ok, I guess." Much to the dismay of my ever fleeting comfort, he squeezed past me, his tall body brushing closely against mine. His hand on my elbow, he quickly apologized although completely insincere as his eyes twinkled playfully. I frowned, ready to walk out the door if anything more uncomfortable took place. He disappeared down the hall. Just then a soft bluesy sort of music started to play. My eyes rolling, I thought, *wow is this guy for real?*

He came back carrying a cute little espresso in hand with a freshly clipped rose on the side. Butterflies made a miraculous return from death and I smiled again shyly. "That is so lovely and I don't even know your name!" He laughed a deep, yet solid laugh and said, "Elias is my name. What a delight to meet you my dear!" Taking my hand in his, he kissed it with all the chivalry I thought men only possessed in long days past.

Going back and lifting the microscope, he held out his hand again. Another kiss I thought: *Oh no! Wait. He wants the gold!* Very audaciously, I turned my back and secretly took out the small velvet pouch wherein the stones resided. I carefully poured them into his hand. He gently placed them under the lens and moaned a "mmhmm" of approval. After what seemed like close to thirty minutes, he turned his back, pouring the stones back into the velvet pouch. We sat down and he folded his arms and crossed his legs as if to relax and say the verdict like a doctor in a clinic. He spoke of the rarity of the stones, the difficulty to say exact quotes because of their small size and the varying of gold prices. "If I had to guess, I would say possibly fifty pounds for each one." My mind thought a hundred thoughts at once. More than I expected, due to the small size of the stones. When I find the parents of these little fellows, I could very well be richer than I had hoped. Elated with the result, I started to pack up my bags, the adrenaline pumping. I wanted to get digging in the cave.

I extended my hand in thanks to Mr. Charming Elias and opened the door to leave down the skinny hallway. He said, "Hope to see you in the near future my dear. Have a lovely day." He shut the door behind me and I was left to make my way down the dim lit hall and out to my adventure. I dropped one of my bags and while it was grounded, I paused to have a quick peek at the stones. Such exciting news, I thought.

I opened the velvet purse carefully. Wait. What was this? Inside the dark velvet it was usually hard to spot the tiny gold stones, but shining out from inside were two bright pearls. OH NO! My head went funny. I dumped the pearls into my hand and felt the light weight of them. Looking closely, the white was chipped off in places, revealing cheap plastic. THAT JERK! No way was he going to steal my gold! Anger flooded my being as I stomped quickly back to the office door and turned the handle. Finding out it was locked, I pounded the door. Peering through the glass, I could see no one; no Elias full of lies and fake charm.

I heard a noise that did not sound like voices but more like grunting, snorting and such. Thinking of pounding so hard the glass might even break, I looked above to see an alarm and a CCTV camera. Oh, I was enraged. He took me for a fool and a fool I turned out to be.

I saw something pass along the shadows in the back.

Pressing my face against the dirty glass window, I could not believe my eyes. PIGS. About a half a dozen sloppy, disgusting swine came out from the back room. The largest one had a tie in its mouth, chewing it up like candy. Yes, it was Elias' tie that he had been wearing only a moment ago. The swine knocked over the quirky old items all around the shop. I could not believe my eyes. What had just happened?

What was going on? I shouted, "Elias, GET OUT HERE NOW!" Anger still boiled in my blood. What an idiot to let animals inside his shop! When I shouted the name again, the large pig waddled over in a strange kind of way, dropping the tie out of his mouth. The damn creature smiled. Yes, I am perfectly aware of how ridiculous that sounds. The pig smiled. Opening his mouth, he had my two stones on the tip of his daft looking, dirty little tongue. I don't even know if he chewed but he sure did swallow. He let out a grunt and they all began to laugh. I felt like I was going mad. Certain of what I saw, I just picked up my things, dropped the pearls at the door and ran out in tears.

Chapter 17

Instead of taking the train to the cave, I felt deflated and decided to go home. I was shaken and upset that I had lost my nuggets and all the hard work was for what? Would the treasure ever be found or was this all a waste of time? Arriving home in the daytime was strange for me.

I was sad but not tired. I sat down and glanced at the case in front of the fireplace. My precious violin was another special thing to me. At least it was not gone. I bent over and unzipped the case, revealing the crimson red velvet bed it laid on. Before another tear had fallen, I played a painfully mournful tune. Often my songs sounded as if they might have been composed in the courts of a Jewish synagogue. I loved the minor notes that soothed my soul's lament. "Things have to change; it has to get better. God please let them get better," I prayed.

The phone rang. "Hello?"

"Hi Honey." My mother's voice was a welcome sound. "Are you there, Letta?" The tears choked me and my voice was not volunteering.

"Honey, you ok?" You have been on my heart and I have been praying for you. "Don't let go of God, Letta. He has such good things for you."

I grunted a *yes*.

"Remember what your daddy used to say. From the minute you entered our house, we knew God had big things in store for you! You are our trooper!"

"I remember mom. I love you."

That call was like chicken soup when you have a nasty cold. She was the only one who could make me believe things could possibly turn around and surprise us all.

It was getting dark, so I ran a bath and lit the candles. Calming down was a wise choice after today. I sipped Chamomile tea and watched the two stars shooting all around. They bounced around the house creating little flecks of stardust as the dance concluded. Their beauty was uplifting and hard for me to describe. Quiet descended and all became still. Peace came from the heavens, and I know it had come at the beckoning of my mother's request.

Chapter 18

The weeks went by, the season began to change, and a warm breeze came by to visit the island. I had still been visiting the cave, although less and less often. Having nothing to show for all the intense work I had done my enthusiasm had waned. The countless hours of labor had taken a toll on my body. My hands had become dry and cracked making it hard to enjoy my violin playing with ease. I soaked them in an herbal solution warmed with green tea.

There came a timely invitation to a wedding and I was asked to play my violin in the rejoicing. The groom, a friend, was one who walked above the clouds. I imagined that his bride might have been born inside those walls of cloud clear beauty. The man wore regal in the way his face was etched. The words that rolled off his tongue flew a flag that was purple in hope. Both were colored purple and smelled of ancient days, encasing new seasons not yet seen. Sometimes it is the kindred spirits that we meet along the way that make the days sing louder. The pleasure would be mine to play at this joyous occasion. The day arrived. With pleasure it arrived! Sitting in the old church, my anticipation was like a magnet causing me to arrive earlier than arranged. I had been concerned in finding the church as my direction skills leave something to be desired. Sitting inside the sanctuary, the age of the building dared me to take out my violin. If I did not comply, the building would have mourned at a missed opportunity to caress its old ears.

Oh the acoustics! It was like the sound of heaven on earth. The strings rang out vibrato on each note as it echoed throughout the building.

I wondered what it felt like to be related to someone. Was there an underlying vibe that you came from the same people? The same curvy bend in the roots of your tree. Did the roots intertwine so you could feel the connection? From time to time I nursed that curious thought.

People had been arriving, and I was dowsing my bow in rosin getting ready to play at any given moment. Just then my hands seized up and instead of dropping my instrument, I held on so tight I thought it might break. Sweat began to bead my brow. *Not now!* I thought.

All that digging had done me damage and for what? It was then in an instant that the sound I heard next was like ointment to my hands. A piano melody echoed out with confidence and a sound I had never heard. The service was over and everyone had left. I began to pack up my things. As I returned to the sanctuary to lift my violin stand, I heard the piano playing a familiar lullaby, "Little star, Little star." I looked up on the stage. Oh my heart! The cutest little boy, maybe around the age of six, was playing the keys of that piano. Sitting high, feet swinging, and his chubby little fingers playing the tune perfectly.

He was dark skinned like me, with stardust on his brow. I went up and sat on the bench next to him. I was almost hypnotized by the tone of his excellent skill that far surpassed his age. Ever so slowly he stopped playing, but not all together. He still constructed a pristine new song with one hand, while taking my hand in the other. As soon as he touched me I knew; I understood the feeling of being related to another human being. He stopped playing the piano and put his other hand on mine. He looked in my eyes, and as he did I was thinking of the many things I wanted to ask him. He said these words as he carefully slipped something into my hand: "Sis, you need to stop your search. You are worth discovering." Then quicker than I thought possible, he jumped down off the bench and walked out the front of the church.

I opened my hand and inside was a folded up piece of black paper. I gently unfolded it and my eyes filled with tears. A childish drawing of a star with a tiny nugget of gold glued to the center of the star. I quickly re-folded the paper as my tears splashed off the drawing smearing a star corner ever so slightly. I ran outside to see the precious tiny boy. I yearned to understand how he had become the owner of gold. I wanted to thank him. He was nowhere to be seen.

Chapter 19

The gold nugget was on the kitchen table as I looked at it through my old microscope. It was a wee bit larger than the ones I had discovered at the cave months past. Just as I was about to hide it back into the velvet pouch a tap came at the door. It was not a knock but more like a tap, perhaps with a cane or something similar. My curiosity sparked as I glanced out the window before reaching the door. I opened the door to find no one in sight. Hmmm. Was this a prankster trying to get me annoyed? Shutting the door loudly, it was the back door that had a tap next. I was now frustrated. I opened the door to see what mischief the prankster was looking for. Again, there was no one to be seen.

I went outside to look around the back. They should not have been able to open the gate from the outside. The gate was secure and intact when I heard the sharpest "Caww!" I felt a rush of wind and jumped back to see the largest eagle I had not even known to exist. Now as previously mentioned, in regard to a certain duck, I am not at ease with birds. Feathered winged creatures cause much anxiety to bubble up, dictating my nerves to unsettle. Swoop! Down it flew, nearly brushing its majestic wings against my face.

Panic set in as I reached for the door handle. I felt my

feet lift off the ground and my sweatshirt tighten as this giant eagle clutched me in its talons. I forgot to mention that I am terrified of heights as well, so at that point I blacked out all together. The next thing I remember was feeling thorns mixed with fur all around me. It was dark and it smelled of stinking wet dog. While I remember what happened, logic and real life argued out the chances in my head. I placed my hands on the ground to support myself in standing up but the sharpness of the floor made it impossible. I saw what looked like feathers and woolly looking fluff. Where was I?

I looked up and it seemed to be a round open roof above me. Looking around, I realized it was a circular room. There were no doors and no windows, just darkness. All of a sudden I heard it again, the sound of wings so close! I felt paralyzed with fear and actually held my breath frozen into utter silence. The room started to shake and I thought it must be an earthquake. No. It was then that I saw the massive bird land. Its talons curled over the roof of the building. I thought I was ready to pass out again.

"Letta, it's me!" Oh my goodness. Just as I was convinced of my last minutes on earth, about to be devoured by a giant eagle, I knew that voice. "Sarah?"

Sarah, who got called Dottie for short, was a dear friend to me. In fact she was my very first friend in N. Ireland. The first day I arrived in the country, I was brought to her house to be introduced. Sarah is such a darling, tenderhearted but refreshingly honest. The thing I appreciated about her the most was her capability to challenge me with brutal honesty but she serves it with loyal friendship and love. It was like serving brussels sprouts in the most dainty china dish with a little French dessert fork to make it look divine.

As delightfully comforting as it was to hear her voice, why was it coming from an eagle?

"Sarah?"

The bird looked into my eyes. I felt calm rush over me, mixed with petrified confusion.

"Letta, I am here to reveal something that will help you find what you are searching for. Since its better that you just observe, your voice has been silenced for the next wee while."

Sure enough, I tried to speak and nothing came out. With one swift swoop, I was lifted onto the eagles back. Scared and thinking of the last time I was flying with the bird, I tried to scream and wriggle off. Too late; we were off. This time I was not as scared. For some unknown reason, a calm came over me minutes before we left.

"I need to show you something Letta."

I could see the Mountains of Mourne; they were so small and we were so high. Flying with ease through the clouds, I sensed my heart fill with excitement. We were nearly above the clouds when I suddenly noticed that we began taking a nosedive at lightning speed. I closed my eyes and gripped her feathers.

It was the wet that startled my eyes open. I was feeling cold water like a shower over me. We were passing by a waterfall. It was the most beautiful sight, colored bright blue with gold rushing through it. It was beyond anything I had ever seen. Just glorious!

"Look straight ahead, Willetta."

I looked and saw that the waterfall was hiding the mouth of a cave. I had so many questions. Trying to speak, I motioned, pointing my finger to my mouth.

The eagle continued, "I am sorry; it's time to listen and observe. This is the other side--the other opening to your hidden cave. The treasure you seek is just after you enter this waterfall."

My friend, she knew! How did she know what I had been doing? How did she know all about the treasure? I began to look around trying to see if the surroundings looked at all familiar. No, nothing looked like the area where my cave resided.

All at once, out flew from inside the cave and right underneath the waterfall, two most royal eagles. They flew in perfect harmony, gliding, almost dancing in the air. As soon as they spoke, I recognized the voice of my Irish parents. But as they spoke sacred words of wisdom above us, out of their mouths dropped nuggets of gold bigger than any I had seen before!

My Irish parents, as I so graciously donned them, had

met my parents and me when we came over for my wedding. They opened up their home and housed us, ran us from here to there helping to organize last minute wedding details. They were lovingly wise people and they told my mother and father they would look after me here in this new country. They kept their word.

Now, just as quickly as they had appeared, they disappeared high above the clouds. I held the golden nuggets in my hand and feeling the weight of them, I longed to see in past the waterfall.

"Willetta, we need to leave now."

Before I knew it, we were in the air and flying higher than we had before. All I saw was green below. Having to grasp on for dear life was my primary concern, but soon I noticed that I no longer held the gold. Nose diving into the trees, I became aware that the room I had been in was nothing more than a nest. A nest!

Sarah gently set me in, pulling some fluff out as she invited me to get some rest. Tomorrow would be extremely busy and we would not have a lot of time. I was so excited! I knew she loved me and would probably take me to collect as much gold as we both could carry. Thinking how much easier life would be, I drifted off to sleep, dreaming of success; the treasure finally found.

I opened my eyes, getting a waft of the most delicious scent. Was that bacon? What? Was I still asleep? I am sitting in a nest, yet I know I smell bacon. The nest shook and was weighed down at one side, tipping ever so slightly as the massive eagle perched on the edge. I sighed not being able to ask her for some of what was smelling delicious as my voice had still disappeared.

"I am sure you are hungry Letta," said the eagle with the voice of my dear friend. Of course I was. What a silly thing to say! Ravenous in fact. "Where is that bacon?" My tummy complained in place of my voice.

"Willetta, you need to learn some valuable lessons today. You have some choices ahead of you that only you can make."

A smaller eagle came into my sight and something was dangling out of its mouth. It was a thick ripped piece of flesh, bloody and absolutely vile looking. As the small eagle got closer, I realized the gorgeous smell was coming from this flesh.

"Everything is not actually what it seems," said Sarah. "The idea you had in your mind, before you actually saw what the flesh looked like, conflicted. The fact that I am an eagle and still your very dear friend, conflicts as well. So many things that we SEE are not truly seen, Letta. You say that you believe in God. Yet He has been trying to get through to you for some time now."

"You are here in Northern Ireland for a specific purpose and reason. You tend to attribute it to mistakes and bad choices, feeling stuck between here and home. You have allowed a little guilt in and you choose to nurse that guilt, blaming yourself for not living closer to your mother, especially now that your father is gone. Guilt is something not seen with your eyes, yet it colors your life and your choices. Living out that example is like a vacuum to stars; it saps all the sparkle and stardust out of them."

My facial expression showed I had decided to put up my defenses. I could not speak, but I sure could give a look to get across my disagreement. Who was she to say that to me? She obviously did not understand my struggle.

The majestic eagle continued on, "Ok Letta, look, you know I love you. I am telling you what I know but it is all up to you. It's your choice to make. You have so much within you. I can see it. I love you."

With that she hopped off the edge of the nest, and I'm not sure where she went. I didn't really even care. She obviously knew about the gold. So how could she think I was not doing my best? I was trying so hard to gain success and make life easier.

Interrupting my thinking, a massive eagle flew above the nest, flapping its wings so hard I had to close my eyes, shut tight. The gust of wind forced my body to rise into the air and I tumbled about like a leaf. Not sure of what was going on, I tried to scream out "Sarah!" but nothing came out. Before I could realize it, I was on the edge of the nest teetering off and nearly losing my balance. I turned around to look for Sarah so I could climb onto her back for help. She made eye contact with me. Her eyes looked sad yet more loving than ever before. With her head, she leaned up against me, pushing me over the edge of the nest.

Tumbling off the edge, gravity in its demanding insistence, pulled me downwards to the death of me, I thought. Just as I questioned the motive of Sarah's betrayal, I also remembered her advice. As I hit off a branch, seeing the rocks below, I said, "Jesus please!" and my voice was louder than I recalled ever hearing it before.

As quickly as I said it, translucent wings spread out. From somewhere inside of me they came. Translucent in appearance, the power they held surpassed my comprehension. I willed them to move up and down as quickly as I could. Just before my great demise, the wings obeyed. I began to fly so close to the ground that the dust blinded my vision yet my wings swept me higher. Soon, I was so high that I could see the other eagles flying--gliding next to me. Their wings looked different from mine. The ones I had seemed to come from the very center of my core, somewhere deep within. I followed the largest eagle and realizing it was Sarah, I tried to fly closer beside her. I think she was a bit surprised to see that I had caught up with her; she looked over and began to descend to our destination. As quickly as we landed, she rose into the air, leaving me behind.

My feet on solid ground, my legs began to shake. I then realized we were back at my house. All of a sudden, I was standing beside the back door where this unusual adventure had begun. Amazed at all that had just happened, I found myself thanking God. My spirit felt awe, not surprise. With quick thoughts of all that had gone on, my head was still questioning and craving what I could *see* and all that was real.

I went inside and lay down on my bed. I am pretty sure I slept for two days straight.

Chapter 20

My phone awakened me and I could see it was Leigh calling from the States. Her pretty face smiling over the phone, she greeted me with our usual, "Hey baby!"

"Hey baby!" I responded.

We had been friends for such a long time. She was at the internship where I had made many wonderful friends. We talked of our busy days, chasing stars, and watering their growth.

Leigh was such a wise soul; she had a mother heart of the church that I never saw in anyone before. She saw the church as a bride and she took delight in all the wedding preparations.

"Letta, I had a dream about you last night and it left me wondering how church was going for you?"

"Mmmm, I have not really been going. I have been too busy these days," I replied sheepishly, knowing this would not meet her approval.

"Oh baby, I love you but you know we all need good leadership and family in our life. That is how God designed it."

"I know, you are right," I responded, hearing the wisdom and truth in her appeal. It was that simple encouraging yet exhorting advice that got me up for church the next morning. As soon as I entered through the doors, I felt as if I entered a house warming party. I was back home, right where I belonged, finding people that would end up loving me for who I was. Even though I did not realize just how lost I was at the present time, some of them noticed. They loved me anyway and accepted me into the family. Each week that I went, the Pastor brought a message that seemed to be intertwined with directions almost like a map. More like satellite navigation, his messages made my eyes more clear every time. I felt as if I was getting closer and closer to something I needed, something the very depths of me craved. I was home.

Chapter 21

An envelope came through my door one evening. With curious anticipation, I opened it to find a letter and inside the letter was a map. The letter said this:

Darling Daughter,
Your Daddy asked me to send you this map before he died. He expressed the importance
of the date on which it should be sent. I know this will come as a shock to your system.
Your Father loved you so very much. I know that the Holy Spirit will lead and guide you.
Always remember that God's Holy Word is a lamp to your feet and a light for your path.
I love you so much Honey.
Your, Mommy

I took out the map and unfolded it ever so very gently. It was a detailed map describing exactly how to get to the other side of the cave. It was the cave where I had seen the waterfall mysteriously located. I could hardly believe my eyes! How did he know? My dad knew just what I needed. God must have shown him before he left this earth.

My heart filled with memories of how my dad was so patient with me and my lack of directional skills. I remembered how, when I started to drive, I used to get lost all the time. Dad took time to get out the map and even write out more simple and detailed directions. *Turn left here, then make a right after the stop sign.* He was very patient with my lack of knowing. Tears filled my eyes at the line he drew out on the map with hand drawn stars and arrows marking out the specifics to the destination. I looked at the date on the calendar and it read November 10. I wondered about the date my mother had mentioned dad had described. What was its significance?

I began to quickly pack all the necessary tools into my bag. I prepared some food and everything I would need for the next day's excursion. This was it! If my dad had made the effort to have this map sent, I would get there as soon as I could. I prayed for good weather for the following day. I knew it would be an extremely important day.

It was November 11 and I started my journey at 5am. I wanted to have enough time to arrive before starting the tedious work ahead. I made it about halfway through the journey when it started to rain. Being used to the quick change of weather in this country, I unpacked my rain gear and layered it all on. I was frustrated that I had forgotten to bring waterproofing for the map my dad had carefully created. The map was very detailed and one wrong turn could lead me into a field of cows.

The rain began to get much heavier and I started to doubt the accuracy of my reading and interpretation of the map. Proceeding to walk along a beautiful yet soggy green valley, I saw someone walking a massive and thoroughly soaked dog. They were heading towards me and as much as they might question my destination, I thought it wise to ask for help.

The man greeted me: "Hi ya. Are ya all right, hey?"

I thought by the accent he was a true country gent. I smiled and replied, "Hi ya. Yes. I was wondering if you could point me in the direction of the Shen Lough?"

"Oh aye, that lough might soon be flooding over love. I would be careful like." He pointed his finger east, and I smiled as it confirmed that I was headed in the right direction.

"Aye, if ya head over that way, it'll get ya over to the lough. Are ya tryin' to catch some fish today; are ya love?" he said with a wink and a smile.

I smiled my biggest smile in return, thanking him and walking on. Turning my head in his direction, I waved and said, "Cheerio!" Very hard to beat the friendly nature of the country folk or small town living!

Rising out of the valley and heading up a rolling green hill, the view was truly breathtaking. I sat down for a few minutes as the rain eased and the sun brightened its rays over the hills' beauty. I studied the map and calculated that it was not much further at all. I was to head into the forest and come to a slight opening where the waterfall was meant to be.

My bags felt heavier with each step I took. All the trees started to look the same and as anxiety threatened to take over, I asked God for clarity. It was in that quiet moment I heard the rush of the waterfall carried over on the wind. Listening so carefully and looking at the map to confirm, the arrow and star were marked not too far ahead. This was it!

As adrenaline drew and pushed me forward, I got past the last group of trees. There it was, the waterfall, with the sunlight shining its rays down in all its glory. The sight before me was heavenly; blue and gold shone down throughout the water.

I threw my bags and tools swiftly inside a little gap in the falls. If I could make my way inside the gap as well, it would be a miracle. The river rocks were covered with a slippery, slimy algae. I placed one foot on a steady looking rock, trying to grip it strategically with my toes. Heaving my weight from one foot to the other, I fell into the other side of the waterfall as if it were an elevator door about to close.

It was so dark and drips of water fell around me. I got my bags and unpacked the lamps I had brought. Trying to strike a match in the dark was a difficult undertaking. After about four attempts, I finally got them lit. As soon as the lanterns lit up and started to spread light throughout the caves' inner dwelling, my eyes questioned what unfolded before me.

The brightness of gold and light was reflecting and bouncing off the walls without a clear source. I searched from where the light came. I could not see the source, but oh, the beauty penetrated my very being.

Gasping at hearing footsteps, I grabbed my mining pick in case of danger. Instead of danger from around one of the caves' close bends, came a black adult male. He smiled at me, sweeping all my concerns aside. He was dressed in a fine black tux and the closer he came, the more familiar he seemed. He came and grabbed my hand and pulling me along, I tried to piece the puzzle together of how I knew him. Why was he in this cave? But at the touch of his hand, I knew. I knew he was my brother, the young boy from the wedding; now a man!

He said, "Come on sis," calling me forward. He led me to a wider space in the cave and standing there was the most beautiful grand piano. The piano was the most gorgeous set of keys I had ever seen. It showed a bit of wear, like it had seen many years. On top of it, many candles were lit painting the most scenic of light.

My brother let go of my hand, quickly positioning himself behind the piano bench but still standing up. He had a slight smile on his face like something good was about to happen. He swept his tuxedo tails behind him as if he was about to take the most magnificent seat ever. Before sitting down, he started to unfasten the most uniquely antique gold-strapped watch. As if in a rush, he held it out to me without making contact. I knew he wanted me to come over quickly and take it. I half ran, half skipped, taking the watch from his extended grip. It was then he looked at me and said, "This is for you; it is TIME."

Without giving me time to respond, he sat down on the bench, pulling it close to the piano as he began to play. The sound he played on each note of the keys caused my spirit to soar. I fell to my knees, nearly fainting. The beauty was too much for me to bear. The music began to swell and crescendo into a classical song. The melody echoed off of each wall, entangling grief and happiness. It was as if my father had just died and yet my baby had just been born and set into my arms. I became aware that the watch began to tick a little bit faster, vibrating ever so slightly in my hands. Not wanting to drop it, I fastened it on my wrist. It looked a little large, and as I looked at my brother, he smiled and played on. He nodded his head up to the roof of the cave, inviting me to see the wonder above.

"Look sis, look up now!" I raised my head to look up at the ceiling but what I saw was open sky with stars filling it like sand on a beach. Never did I think that amount of stars existed. Then he switched the music and quieted down to the most beautifully familiar lullaby. The intricate detail he added to the song was absolutely stunning. Just when I thought my eyes and ears could take no more beauty or I would pass out completely, it was then I saw the angels. They appeared to be angelic beings that you would see painted on the walls of a cathedral in Rome. They wore flowing silk robes, almost Victorian in style, with sweeping hair. They floated along, hovering and sitting around the top of the cave. It seemed to be too many to count, and I suddenly thought I must have slipped and fallen and this must be Heaven!

My brother must have known what I was thinking and he shook his head as if to say, "No, Letta, this is real."

With a smile, he played on. I felt the watch steady its pace. My brother stopped smiling and a slight wave of seriousness flashed across his face. Glancing up at the angels, he began to sing out as if he was leading a choir and they would know how to follow.

"Hope, built to be a bridge and strength for a new life!" the song went on and the angels took over the chorus.

Such voices I had heard not. Shaking my head in utter disbelief and amazement, I heard my brother say, "Letta, I believe in you."

With those words, I appeared to be in a different place all together. I was in a bathroom! I looked around and it seemed to be marked "disabled with wheelchair access" and had a bed sheet for a door. Confused, I tried to understand what was going on. I could see people walking by. I saw one lady peering through the sheet and it hit me that I must be in a hospital. As I sat there perplexed, I saw the same woman walk by and I noticed she seemed somewhat familiar. She held a little baby in her arms. I looked at the sink next to me and in front of the sink was a small red car seat and inside of it was a tiny little bundle all wrapped up. My memory flooded with recognition that I had just given birth to my first son! Love and excitement washed over me. I could just about see his face because he was wrapped up tightly with such protecting garments.

I heard footsteps again and having gathered myself together, I lifted the car seat and headed towards the sheet. I pulled it open to find the same girl with her baby passing by. She was a nice looking Hispanic girl with half her hair up in a messy ponytail. She seemed like she was dressed in sort of 80's style attire. She smiled at me and motioned me to bring my face and listening ear close.

She whispered, "We have to go quickly; you're already late."

My only concern was my son and I sensed that my time at the hospital was done. She started walking quickly down the hall. I followed without hesitation as the familiar feeling of knowing her gave me peace. Soon we had entered another building. It was some sort of modern arena or hall with tiered seating reaching up quite high. The place was buzzing with all sorts of people. The girl rushed on and I stood there taking it all in.

As I was looking across the vast seating, I heard music.

I had heard the sound before; the orchestra was tuning up in preparation for their concert. The string section harmonized the A string with the D string on their instruments and on and on they went. I saw across the space that there seemed to be a few people I might recognize. I moved towards them, thinking of the questions I needed to ask. But before I could reach them, a handsome black man approached me. He seemed concerned yet happy to see me. He embraced me with a familiarity that proved we had embraced many times before. He looked around me and said, "Honey, where is the baby?"

Tears streamed down my face as my heart sank. I thought I had him! Where was my baby? I remembered carrying him and setting him down while I was lost in my thoughts inside this big concert hall, trying to figure out where I was.

The man gently cupped my face in his hands and wiped away my tears. He kissed me lightly and said, "It's fine; he will be here somewhere."

He quickly rushed off in search of the child and I began to jog around the circular level of the hall. I could see people taking their seats as if the concert was about to start. I did not care that I was running around like a maniac with people muttering for me to move. I needed to find my baby! Having only just been born, he needed me. How could I be so careless?

I had come up to the center of the building when I saw

an elevator. As I pressed the button to go up to the next floor, a few others gathered around talking and wanting to get to their seats. The lift was taking a long time but when it opened, I saw the Hispanic girl inside. Her eyes met mine and as I tried to get in, she placed her hand on my elbow while still holding her baby with the other. She ushered me out and said, "Those lifts are not reliable, so follow me. I will show you the stairs."

I told her I was looking for my baby and she responded, "I know your husband and he met me down on the other level and asked me to help you both look for your son."

I was so relieved; the more help the better! My body ached climbing the stairs. For such a big hall the stairs looked like they had not been used for years. Mice and dirty old boxes cornered the steps. Confused as to what was going on, I cast the observations to the side because I had one mission: My baby needed me! I feared the worse. We reached the next floor and we split up and went opposite directions. I heard the orchestra begin to start. Not caring, I stepped on toes and could hear people getting annoyed as I rushed by. I was approaching a sound desk. I could see the men hard at work to get the stage to its right sound. As I was about to pass by, I looked and saw a bit of red. It was the car seat! Oh my heart! I saw my son and noticed that a small pile of papers was on top of him. Anger bubbled up in me and I took the paper off and saw my baby's face. He was fine and sleeping. I lifted the car seat, hoping to go find my husband and the girl to let them know all was well.

As I turned to walk away, a man grabbed my arm. He was not happy that I held the papers in my hand.

"Excuse me," he said, in a tone of condemnation mixed with annoyance. "I need that music!"

His tone was firm and assured. He held his hand out for me to return the music promptly. I was not amused. Who did he think he was to pile music on top of my baby? His pompous attitude boiled my blood. I hooked the handle of the car seat in the crook of my arm and with both my hands I threatened to rip the music in two. It was at that flash of temper and sudden threat that the entire team of men stopped what they were doing and stared at me in shock. In my anger I didn't really care.

The man said, "You wouldn't dare, do you know how important that music is?"

My response shocked my own ears! I uttered such profanity that I wasn't even sure of the meaning. I wanted to prove that I was not scared of these men who didn't take notice of my newly born son. I tore the pile of music in two; shock and unnecessary horror filled each face.

I thought to myself, "It's only music!"

I had not noticed that one of the men had pressed a button and I saw security men rush in from the hall. There must have been a dozen officers rush at me and start guiding me away. They were not happy and the severity of my decision hit me like a ton of bricks. Uh-Oh I thought, what was the big deal? Surely they were just going to kick me out. They grabbed my arms so hard that it nearly lifted me off the ground. I expressed my unhappiness, asking where they were taking me. They ignored me and only spoke to each other.

I saw my husband approach and I quickly passed him our baby. He tried to reason with the security men and they ignored him and rushed me on. I saw him stop to comfort the baby and it was then that I felt tears approaching my eyes. I would not cry; they could not see me cry! They brought me into another room. It seemed to be a large courtroom. The men pushed me past many people, all standing and staring at me. I took it all in, feeling a swell of hatred decorate the room from these people.

The room was filled to the brim with nearly all Caucasian people who never intimated me until now. They all seemed to look at me with such hatred. I did not understand what I had done so wrong. Why was I brought here? What was going to happen? I was ushered roughly past the people all looking at me, talking and shouting, pointing and accusing. A fear gripped the very innermost corners of my being. I suddenly ripped free and started running towards the nearest exit. I was met by groups of people pushing at me and scratching at my body. When I tried to see over the crowd, I saw my friend who was like my sister. Shouting her name, I saw my husband with a terrified look, coming towards her. I watched between the shoulders of people that he handed her the baby. She was speaking to him but I could not make out what they were saying.

I felt my arms being grabbed and turned to see a few security men angrily beside me. They spoke to me with utter disgust and led me away to the front of the room. I was told to sit at a table facing the front. As I tried to take my seat amidst the chaos and pushing and shoving of the guards, I bumped into a man in front of me. Three times I bumped into him. He was a tall man, quite skinny, but with eyes full of disdain. I apologized to him for bumping him but he looked away and smiled with pleasure written on his mouth. He took a step up to what seemed like a small podium that would be a witness stand. He started to speak as the guards sat me down directly in front of him. The people hushed slightly but the underlying murmur was still going on.

The man started to speak. "This is exactly why these niggers should still be our slaves!" he shouted towards the people.

At his words, an entire row of men and woman stood to their feet and cheered. I was shocked! What was going on? How was he allowed to say such a thing? Completely confused, the fear that filled me caused my face to set hard as stone. I was frozen in disbelief.

I looked around the room and began to notice a few

familiar faces: people that I had not had good encounters with in the past; people I never wanted to see again. The terror gripped me and shame filled me. I felt the sick rise in my throat. I leaned over to one side and threw up. As I was leaning over, I heard a familiar voice start to speak. I wiped my mouth and quickly looked at the stand.

"This woman is despicable."

He continued to paint a murky picture with vivid detailing that caused the shame to outweigh my fears. Groups of people began to cheer and titter with laughter as he spoke of my indiscretions. I looked through the crowd. Over to the left hand side of the crowds I saw a small group of people I knew. I was horrified, yet grateful, to see my Pastor, my mother, my husband and a few friends. They had a look of disbelief at what they were hearing. I felt shame like blood running through my veins. I thought these things were hidden forever. Why did these people come forth to expose my secrets and his added lies? I had made mistakes, but who hadn't? I never expected them to be told and shouted boldly in front of everyone.

The man, who was still spelling out intimate details of my past, got a perverted smile on his face and turned his eyes towards me. A group of men, about eight in total, got up from their seats and started surrounding my table. I could sense the harm they intended me, sexual in nature.

All of a sudden and over the muttering of the crowd, I

heard my mother's voice shout, "Stop! NO! Don't let them touch her!"

Her voice was quickly drowned out by laughter and mocking. The crowd reveled in what was about to take place.

One large man lifted me out of my seat and threw me onto the table. The crowd cheered the men on, raising their fists and shaking them in the air. I closed my eyes because I knew what was coming, I heard the belts unbuckling and zippers being undone. Surely people would not just stand by and let this take place. I felt a man grip my thighs with such force his fingernails dug into my skin. He laughed, my eyes squeezed shut and my jaw clenched fiercely I braced myself for the violence to come. The cheers were loud but all of a sudden silenced by a sharp thud of a gavel. A tallish well built man with a beard, dressed in an odd looking suit, came over and pushed the men to the side. He spoke with a loud voice and told them to take their seats. I quickly scrambled off the table and with one angry shove, the man overturned the table. Everyone grew even quieter.

The man, with added calm in his voice yet still shouted, "I call my client to the stand!"

All eyes were on me. My eyes ventured back to this man in his suit to see him nodding me forward towards the stand.

Cautiously, I proceeded to take the stand. In front of me I saw nasty smirks and the evil I felt in the room caused me to sway ever so slightly. Taking hold of the sides of the stand, I went over the thoughts in my head. What was I to say? I did not know what words might flow out of me. I knew the bad I had done yet most people do bad things in their life. I looked at the man I assumed to be my lawyer and he looked at me with the compassion that I longed to have spread like a domino effect through the crowd.

As I began to speak, I felt the heat of anger stain my lips. I began to utter words in my defense, justifying and victimizing myself. I shouted and blamed, accusing and maiming the ones in my life who had let me down since birth. Abandoned and abused, I had been so confused and it caused me to lie and steal from those who trusted me. I explained to the crowd in detail how each wrong turn I had taken was due to the shaken walls of the womb in which I was conceived.

The faces staring back at me grew in anger. Why could they not understand? I was wrong in my actions but reasons were reasons. I stopped talking and looked to the back of the room. I saw my sweet friend starting to lift my baby boy out of his sleep. It was then I saw what he had so tightly wrapped him. It was an unusually rare bit of wax! My friend looked at me as the crowd began to murmur. They began with taunts, boos, and threats. I motioned to my friend to take him out, to leave. She seemed perfectly calm as she peeled the wax from around my son. The intensity began to grow as people started to rise from their seats. Some lifted knives; others had guns. I knew what was coming. The hate had created a storm cloud. It blew closer in. Trying to see through the people, I saw what she was doing. I gripped tightly to the stand and kept staring. She had formed a large star out of the wax. Having tied the star with string to the handle of the car seat, she launched him into the air.

I screamed, "No, not my baby!" assuming he would fall to the floor. Instead the ceiling opened up and the star drifted gently yet swiftly into the sky filled with stars. The sky looked like it did when my brother was playing his song. Although I heard no music now, only shouts of hatred and judgment from the people. I met the eyes of my lawyer as I stepped off the stand. I mouthed, "I am sorry."

He stood up and set the big table back on its feet. He pulled out my chair and told me to take a seat. My back was to the crowd and I could sense the judgment was about to be called out. I looked around to see a judge but I saw no one in the high seat. Oh, the angry people must be judge and jury I thought. I heard the weapons start to bang. I turned to see the people shouting and in unison they began to bang their weapons and their feet. I cried at the horror I thought they would bring upon me in the next few minutes. I saw my lawyer rush out the nearest exit. He must be leaving to save himself. I did not even blame him. This was all my fault. I hung my head waiting for the first blow.

All of a sudden, as if the radio had been turned on, the

speakers began to play classical music. I lifted my head to see what looked like waiters and waitresses rush in from the same door my lawyer had exited. They came to my table and spread out a white linen tablecloth over its entirety. With the crowd still screaming and shouting, along came my lawyer with a slight grin on his face. He had changed into a tuxedo and carried in large plates filled with food. What? I could not understand. Was this my last meal before being brutally killed?

The waiters kept coming in and out of the door. Back and forth they came with roasted duck, pig and steak--a massive feast that smelled divine. As they rushed about, I noticed one of the waiters had silk coming out from underneath his uniform. It was then that I looked closer at the faces of the staff and I recognized them as the angels that had been singing with my brother. Oh my! I could not fathom what was going on. The cold liquid running into my lap brought me back to what was happening right in front of me. He who I assumed to be my lawyer was pouring out wine into a glass in front of me. He smiled as he kept pouring while it overflowed all around me.

With that he spoke with confidence that calmed me: "Willetta, do you realize that mercy triumphs over judgment? I have prepared this feast for you in the midst of these your enemies. I have paid the bill for all this food and I want you to enjoy it. You are not to worry but just eat ok? It's all for you."

With that, he took off his fancy jacket and went out into the crowd. I screamed as I saw the crowd attack him without a second thought. I saw the blood begin to pour off his body as they kicked and stabbed him with all their might. This was my fault. I got up wanting to try and intervene but the angels stepped in to stop me.

"Can't you see what they are doing?" I shouted! "Please, help him! Please!" I begged.

I was met with silence. With every blow it seemed like the crowd got smaller. After the murderers cheered in celebration, they dissipated, wandering out of the court. Emptied out, the room felt much bigger. I ran over to the body of this man, this man who had saved my life. His body had been so brutally disfigured that I could not even see if it was his face or the back of his head. I knelt down in the blood, watering it with my tears. I looked up into the sky, expecting the stars to still be lighting up the sky. Instead I saw the sky was black and simply three exquisitely bright shooting stars fly across the sky. I knew those stars were mine. Yet I could take no comfort in them. As my hands dripped blood, I touched the body I felt responsible for killing.

Another hand surprised me as I felt it on my shoulder. I turned to see my brother standing behind me. I stood up, quickly falling into his comforting embrace. "Sis, it's ok. Watch to see what will happen. He did this for you gladly!"

The words my brother said brought confusion. He

reached over, wiping my tears with his fingers. He took me by my limp arm and led me to the back of the room. Since I thought we were leaving, it seemed strange that my brother was walking backwards, looking with wonder at the lawyer's body. I turned to look one last time, feeling like the guilt was strangling me, taking my breath away. I saw the entire angelic group lift his mangled body; and as they did, I saw him transforming before my eyes.

My brother took my wrist in his hand and quickly unclasped the watch. Then he spoke to me in a rushed voice full of excitement: "This is your time. You are discovered!"

Not exactly listening but engrossed in the sight before me, I watched as the angels ascended with my friend the lawyer into the sky. Just as the lawyer stood straight up in the midst of the clouds with the angels flying below, he threw something down to me. As it landed in my hands, I could see it was a massive gold rock. The weight of it was heavy. It began to melt--melting into and all over my hands. The heat was surprisingly subtle. With that, my brother pushed me out the door. With a shove, I was back on the other side of the waterfall.

Rubbing my eyes and not understanding what had gone on, I felt a substance on my hands. My hands were covered in bright gold glittery dust. I bent over the river to see my reflection. My face and my neck also were covered in the gold dust. It was then that I remembered what my brother had said all along, He spoke about me being treasure and being discovered. It came to my mind that this was the start of my adventure. I was saved for a reason--to help other people discover the details of their story. I knew a certain lawyer who could help them come to the sense of their purpose and pay the price and debt of their case. The puzzle came together in my mind--all the pieces falling into place. This was the reason I was in this country.

Chapter 22

Having found the black gold on this Emerald Isle has been such a pilgrimage and it's only just unfolding. The joy I have experienced in discovering such brightness has both baffled and amused me to the core. The joy most definitely outweighs the sorrow. I believe that each person on earth has their own unique story and journey to pursue. Your story may seem more complex or perhaps more simple than mine, but the beauty in my discoveries up until this day is this: I know God, and He will take you by the hand when you ask Him to. He will sweep away the doubt and confusion as to why things have happened in your life. He is strong enough to overturn the table of your enemies. He will rescue you, take you on a grand adventure helping you discover the aim of your purpose, and in that exploration you will find your treasure: who you are and why you are here. He is God of the impossible. A God who sets a banquet and feast before you in front of your worst enemy. God has shown me that He keeps His word. I encourage every single person to wake up to the adventure going on around you and in you. What you might not physically see is not, not taking place. There is so much going on in the unseen realm as well as in the seen. You just have to choose to wake up to it.

Whoever you are,
   wherever residence may be your Emerald Isle,
   and in whatever circumstances you may find yourself,
   rest assured God wants you to find your gold there.